www.twitter.com/iamobsession

https://www.facebook.com/Obsessionthewriter

https://www.facebook.com/I.AM.OBSESSION

Climatic Successions

(A mosaic of broken hearts)

A novelette by Obsession

Chapter One

Brooklyn goes hard

"It really burns my ass when I have to do parents' jobs and raise their kids! Damn that pisses me off!"

Being a kindergarten teacher on the west side of Chicago has proven to be more of a challenge than Brooklyn thought; not because of the children, but because of the parents.

"Let me woosah before I lose my job." Brooklyn closed her eyes and took a deep breath before entering principal Braiden's office.

As usual, Mr. Braiden had on his favorite suit. The powder blue one that looked extremely uncomfortable in certain areas, with the white collar and cuffs. This man is looking like a 70's pimp! I ain't lying, I ain't lying! Brooklyn thought to herself.

"Welcome, Ms. Monroe. Please have a seat so we can get started."

Brooklyn had approached principal Braiden weeks before about having a meeting with the parents of Jayden Claire. Jayden is a feisty, but intelligent young boy who displays an 'I don't give a fuck attitude' at 5 years old. An attitude that will get him nowhere in life…at least that's what Brooklyn believed. She knew by the 'I don't want to be here' look on Jayden's mother's face, it was going to get real ugly, and quick.

"Mrs. Claire, we've asked you to attend this meeting….."

"Mrs. Claire? I ain't married. Just call me Tameka."

Mr. Braiden cleared his throat.

"Okay, Ms. Tameka, we've asked for you to attend this meeting because Ms. Monroe here expressed some concerns about Jayden's behavior and efforts in her class."

Cutting her eyes at Brooklyn, she said,

"Well what the hell is he doing?"

"Well Ms. Tameka, Jayden has been extremely disruptive in class. Jayden throws paper at the other students, blurts out random things when his classmates are reading, etc. He doesn't do his class work nor does he bring back his homework. That's where you come in."

"I work two jobs, so I don't have time for no petty worksheets and shit. This is nothing but kindergarten. This don't even count." Brooklyn sat straight up in her chair.

"Come again?"

Swirling her neck, "I said, this little shit here don't even count. It's just kindergarten."

Mr. Braiden dropped his head because he knew that Brooklyn was about to set it off.

"Let me spank that ignorant statement that just came out your mouth."

Oh shit! Mr. Braiden thought.

"Children learn while in the womb, Tameka. Parents are a child's first and most important teacher that they will ever encounter in life. Its parents like YOU, who make my job a lot harder than it has to be, all because you don't want to do your job as a parent, and participate in your child's educational growth. Just because you are happy with being raggedy, does not mean your son has to be a statistic."

Shifting in her seat, Tameka's eyes became teary as Brooklyn continued.

"I'm so tired of Caucasian and Asian children excelling in academics, while our babies excel in everything but. African Americans need to wake up now, because we are being laughed at and left behind. Tameka if your attitude doesn't improve as a woman and as a mother, then Jayden is going to end up in these streets, jail, or worse…dead." Brooklyn leaned in closer to Tameka. "He doesn't give a damn because you don't give a damn; and why should he care if his own mother doesn't care about his future?"

Enraged, Tameka shot up, her fist clinched and crying.

"This is my goddamn son! I raise him how the hell I want! Maybe I should put him in a school where the teachers don't have so much mouth."

"Ladies let's not go there." Mr. Braiden continued. "We only have Jayden's best interest at heart. We want nothing but for him to reach his fullest potential."

Grabbing her purse, Tameka looked at Brooklyn.

"I don't care what y'all want."

"And that's not the only thing that's apparent, Ms. Tameka." Brooklyn said while opening the office door, "It is also obvious that you don't even care about yourself."

Bumping shoulders with Brooklyn Tameka whispered,

"Fuck you chick."

Brooklyn laughed, "I guess we won't be nominating you for mother of the year."

"Fuck y'all! I'm taking my son out of here!" Tameka yelled over shoulder while walking away.

Massaging his temples, principal Braiden tilted his head back.

"Ms. Monroe tell me why? Just...tell me why?"

"Principal Braiden, you know she needed to be told the truth! Why does she have to ruin that boy's life because she's given up on her own?" Brooklyn asked pleadingly.

"I got you Brooklyn, but you could've been more professional. Instead you lost your temper, as usual, and that's not okay."

"Okay, okay, I'm sorry. But you know how passionate I am about my students...about education period."

Smiling, Mr. Braiden rubs his head.

"Yea I know, that's why you're getting written up and not fired."

"Written up?! She deserved…" Brooklyn covered her mouth in mid-sentence.

"Brooklyn, no back talk, now get out of here and go enjoy your weekend.

"Thank you Mr. Braiden, see you Monday morning."

"Have a good one Brooklyn, and no more meetings for a while okay?"

Brooklyn burst out laughing, "For sure Mr. Braiden, for sure."

Heading out the building, Billups, the janitor, almost breaks his neck to speak to her.

"Have a good weekend Ms. Monroe."

"You too Billups…,"

Giggling, Brooklyn thought to herself, if he didn't look like he just escaped through the Underground Railroad, then maybe I'd give him some play. You see, all of the male teachers and janitors had the hot's for Brooklyn. She was 5'5, chestnut brown, with almond shaped hazel eyes, long brown wavy hair, with high cheek bones, full plush lips, and the perfect shape. Not only was she beautiful, but she was intelligent and ambitious with a down to earth personality. Even being all of that, Brooklyn was single, and had been for the last four years.

"Oh Lord I'm exhausted." Brooklyn mumbled while opening her car door.

"I just want to go home and sleep, but I can't. Ugh why did I promise mom that I would go on this blind date she set up?"

Starting the ignition, she pulled off in thought, wondering if this man that her mother met at the grocery store was 'the one', or would he be another disappointment?

"I guess we will find out tonight, won't we?"

Brooklyn turned up the radio and jammed all the way to her apartment. She didn't even get one foot in the door before her phone rang.

"Geesh! Can I get in the door before people start calling?!"

Tossing everything on the sofa including herself, she flipped open her cell.

"Hello?"

"Hey Ms. Lady, are we still on for the night?"

It was her blind date Kevin. Mmmmm he sounds so sexy, Brooklyn thought.

"Yes, of course we're still on. I'm getting ready now."

"Okay I'll see you at six dear…bye."

"Bye"

I hope he looks as good as he sounds, she said while popping in a Meshell Ndegeocello before hopping into the shower.

"Let me run my fingers through your…dreadlocks! And rub your body doowwwnn."

What am I going to wear? Brooklyn thought while standing in the mirror. After thirty minutes of indecisiveness, she chose a sexy but classy knee length, backless black dress.

"Ahhhh ish! This is my jam right here!"

Slow dancing and singing to herself, "Here I sit outside your door, talk ta meee."

 Interrupted by her cell ringing, she turned down the music.

"Hey there, are you on your way?"

"Eww, this is not dude!"

It was her best friend Derricka.

"Ah shit girl I thought you were Kevin. What the hell do you want?"

"Apparently you did, answering the phone like you work for 1-800-stroky doke!"

They both laughed.

"And you know I called to be nosy! Girl is he fine or what?!"

"He's not here yet, he said he'd pick me up at six." Brooklyn giggled.

"Well hell, its 5:30, he better bring his ass."

Derricka was just as feisty, successful, and beautiful as Brooklyn, but without the temper. She could always find the good in people regardless of their faults.

"I know right! He better not stand me up." Brooklyn said while sliding on the $100 pumps that she brought specifically for this date. Brooklyn and Derricka began talking about the events of the day. Before long it was 6 pm.

"Girl its 6 o'clock and he's not there?" asked Derricka.

"Nope he's not….." Brooklyn heard a car honking.

"Hold up girl, somebody's blowing their horn." Brooklyn looked out the window to see a man leaning against a BMW.

"Derricka, I think this is Kevin and he's driving a BMW girrrl! I gotta go!"

"Okay okay! You better call me BK with all the details."

"I will…bye boo."

Brooklyn hung up, checked herself over once more, and then headed downstairs.

"Oh My God He's fine! Thanks mom!"

Brooklyn stood in the doorway staring at a 6 foot tall, red bone with dimples, clean cut spec of a man.

"Brooklyn stop staring" she mumbled as she walked towards him.

"Brooklyn?"

"Yes I'm Brooklyn. You must be Kevin?"

"In the flesh, let me get the door for you." He grabbed her by the hand and led her to the passenger side. He surprised Brooklyn by buckling her seat belt for her.

"Wow, thank you. No one has ever done that for me before."

He looked her in the eyes and smiled.

"No problem baby."

The car ride was awkwardly quiet, at least to Brooklyn.

"Would you like to hear some music?" Kevin looked over at Brooklyn.

He must have read my mind, Brooklyn thought.

"Sure I would like that."

"Okay let's see what's on the radio."

Kevin skipped past Trey Songz and Erykah Badu, and stopped on Celine Dion.

"Oh my God I love this song."

Kevin turned up the radio and began to lip-sync 'That's the way it is'.

Brooklyn cocked her head to the left and said under her breath, "Is this fool really bumping Celine Dion and singing to it? What in the world?"

They finally pulled up to this popular joint called, 'Aaron's' in downtown Chicago.

"I've been dying to try this place out; I just didn't have anyone to come here with, so I decided for my first time to be with you."

He looked into her eyes, and they simultaneously burst out laughing.

"That was kind of corny, huh?" asked Kevin.

"Yea that was pretty corny."

He took her hand and they walked into Aaron's.

Aaron's was beautiful. It was made up of earth tones with beautiful furniture. A live band play jazz set the mood along with the wonderful art decorating the walls. All Brooklyn could think about was how warm and inviting this place was. After ten minutes of waiting for a table, they were finally seated.

"Hello welcome to Aaron's. I'm Aaron, the owner. Can I start you off with some drinks?"

"Yes white wine will be fine, if that's alright with the lady."

"Yes white wine is good."

"Great! I'll give you time to look over the menu, and in the meantime I'll go get the wine."

"Thank you Aaron." Kevin said while caressing Brooklyn's hand.

"So Ms. Brooklyn, you can order whatever you like, except dessert."

Uh oh he's about to say something nasty, Brooklyn thought.

"And why no dessert Mr. Kevin…," She asked smiling?

"Because we ordered wine, this is not a relationship, it's just a date. You can't have a meal, dessert, and wine, at least not if I have to pay for it."

Brooklyn did a double take.

"Say what?"

"Okay listen", leaning back in his chair, "I ordered wine because that's what I wanted. If you were my girl, then you could have whatever you wanted, but you're not." Brooklyn leaned over the table.

"Okay check this out dude. Do I have lame written across my forehead? Do you see little ass kid written anywhere on my body? SO WHO THE FUCK ARE YOU TALKING TO?! This is why black women date outside of their race, or why women go lesbian, because of raggedy extra super stupid men like you!"

Kevin started to speak.

"Shut your goofy ass up. You don't have a damn thing to say to me brother!"

Heads turned, and people gasped. Aaron ran to their table.

"Excuse me what is the problem?"

"He's a raggedy ass bastard, that's the problem!" Brooklyn took both glasses of water and tossed them on Kevin.

"Aye dude, don't ever in your life call my phone again…EVER!"

Sitting at the table drenched in water, Kevin watched Brooklyn storm out of the restaurant.

An hour later, after a long hot shower, Brooklyn crawled into bed and called her best friend to vent.

"Yea another one wasted my time. I'm so tired of going out with these losers in Chicago. First it was Daryl and his 15 kids that he doesn't claim but they sure in the hell do claim him. Then it was Shawn who forgot to mention that he liked women and men. Oh and let's not forget Marcus. Mr. 'Women belong in the kitchen barefoot and pregnant and not in corporate America', and many more idiots before and after them."

"Yea girl I feel you. Just keep talking to the Lord, it will happen for you…hell for the both of us, hopefully." Derricka laughed out loud, "Girl I can't believe you lit him up like that in that restaurant. I know he was mad as hell."

"Please, I was mad as hell, coming at me like I was a trick or something. I had to let him know."

Derricka laughed.

"Yea I know. That's why I love my Brooklyn. When you snap out, you go hard."

Chapter Two

Stronger than my breeders

"Derri, I wish I could be more forgiving like you; you have a heart of gold."

"Psh! Chile I wasn't born with this heart, I created it."

"You know every time you say things like that I always wonder what you mean." Brooklyn said.

"I mean I know we're best friends and all, but I feel that there's a lot that I don't know about you. Like your childhood for instance, you never talk about it."

Brooklyn waited for Derricka to respond, but she didn't.

"Derricka?"

"Yes BK, I'm here. Listen, I don't talk about my childhood because there's nothing worth mentioning."

"Okay, I'll drop the subject."

"Thank you ma'am."

More silence.

"BK, girl the way that you described Aaron's makes me want to go! So when are you free?"

"Um, how about Tuesday night, around 7 o'clock?"

"Cool. Well let me get off this phone. I have two photo shoots to do. Then I have a meeting, so it's going to be a long day."

"Alrighty Derri, talk to you later."

Derricka hung up the phone with teary eyes.

"Why can't I share my life with my own best friend?"

She wiped her eyes, "I thought I was over that shit. I need a drink."

Derricka went to the kitchen, grabbed a bottle of red wine, and took it straight to the head.

"God, I'm behaving like my father."

Placing the wine back in the fridge, two words echoed in her mind...'My father'.

Derricka is the eldest of four sisters. Her father used to say all the time that she was the prettiest little girl in the world. He always kept his girls in dresses. No pants, no shorts, just dresses. She never understood why, until she was 10 years old. That was the age when their mother went to the store one day and never came back. That was the age when her father started looking at her differently. Angered by his wife's sudden departure, Derricka's father took his wrath out on the girls, especially her. He made her the woman of the house. She was made to cook, clean, wash, bathe, and comb her younger sisters' hair. Every morning, Derricka was made to cook breakfast and to get everybody out the door on time. One night, exhausted from her daily tasks, she headed to the bedroom she shared with her sister. She never made it, because her father called her into his room…

Snapping out of thought, Derricka hadn't realized that she'd left the kitchen and crawled into bed.

"I don't remember coming in here to lie down."

She looked over at the clock on her nightstand; it was a bit after 1 a.m.

"Shit I need to sleep. I need fresh eyes for these photo-shoots.

Derricka Fallon was a well-known fashion photographer. She's worked with top names in the fashion and hip hop industries, and through blood, sweat, and tears, she opened 'Fallon's Photography Studio' on the outskirts of downtown Chicago. As a child, Derricka took an interest in photography when her father burned every last picture of her, her sisters, and their mother. Some days she felt like her parents tried to break her down because they were miserable and pitiful, but they never did, and she promised herself that they never would.

"If I wasn't saved, I'd murder that bastard for what he did to me. And for her..." Derricka's frown deepened at a mental picture of her mother. "I'd just drive by to wherever she is, smack the hell out of her, and then pull off." Derricka pulled the covers over her head and fell asleep.

Chapter Three

Don't want to be a player no more

Thailand Moore was the most sought out massage therapist in the Chicago land. He was a 29 year old standing 6 foot 2, dark skinned with a clean goatee, a cleft in his chin, and a body to die for. It made perfect sense that all of his clients were women. Single women, married women, divorced women, spiritual women, women who all lost their religion at the touch of Thai. His clients nicknamed his hands 'Orgasmic', because he worked their bodies so good that they climaxed. They slipped him their numbers, and made arrangements for private sessions. Thai had everything a woman could ever want in a man; the looks, the charm, the bank accounts. Yes, that's bank accounts with a's'. There was only one thing…Thailand was a player, but could you really blame him? I mean with all that he's working with, he could have any woman that he wants, and he has. Soon that aspect of his life will change.

"Mmmm…Thai go lower baby." Obeying the request of his client, Thai slid his hands down to her lower back and worked her in a slow circular motion. She moaned like they all did, as he traced the lining of her left thigh and began massaging it with long, smooth, strokes.

"Trisha told me you were the bomb and now I can see why." Her breathing became deeper and she began to vibrate, so he pressed harder, and sped up his movement. She clinched the table and verbally assured Thai that she enjoyed his work by releasing a high pitched moan.

Thai smiled and thought to himself, yet another satisfied customer. After cleaning up his work space, Thailand headed to the front desk to check for next day appointments with is receptionist.

"Hey Ms. Lauryn, who's up for tomorrow?"

"Let me check that for you right now Mr. Moore." While waiting for a list of his clientele, he caught a glimpse of a woman walking past his business window.

"God, she's beautiful", Thai whispered.

Lauryn, frowned. "Mr. Moore?"

By this time, Thai had his face smashed up against the window. Rolling her eyes, she repeated.

"MR. MOORE!"

Thailand spun around with a surprised look on his face.

"What's up? Who I got?"

"You have Ms. Livingston at 10 a.m., Ms. Joseph at 12 p.m., and Mrs. Harrison at 2:30 p.m., who's by referral."

Thailand smiled, "I love new clients. Who referred her?"

Lauryn smiled even bigger, "You already know. Trisha!"

Thai narrowed his eyes.

"So are we still on for our private session tonight?"

Lauryn licked her lips, "When have I ever missed an opportunity to feel the touch of the amazing Thai?"

Smirking Thailand said, "Never baby, and you never will. See you tonight, same time…"

Lauryn broke in, "Same place."

Lauryn watched Thailand walk out the door, then shivered.

"That man, that man! God! I'm going to make him mines…watch."

Thailand whipped out the keys to his brand new Mercedes, with the woman he'd seen walking by still on his mind. "Damn she was really pretty. I should've caught her." Putting in his ear piece, Thailand dialed his homeboy's number.

"What's up Ron Ron!"

Aaron laughed, "Why are you so god damn loud man?"

"Dude you already know I have to be heard. I'm Thailand, you know how I do. How is the restaurant going bro?"

"If my best friend would stop by and check it out, instead of serenading different women every night, then my best friend would know how it's going."

"Oh so now I'm just your best friend? We're not brothers anymore? It's like that?!" questioned Thailand.

"Man whatever. You know you're my brother for life, but you have dropped the ball in this friendship. Am I lying?" asked Aaron.

"You're right. I haven't been as supportive as I should be, and you're right about another thing…I have been with different women every night. But that's what I wanted to talk to you about."

There was a brief silence.

With concern in his voice, Aaron spoke, "What's up bro, you good?"

Thailand took a deep breath, "I don't know if I'm good, but what I do know is that I don't want to be a player no more."

Aaron coughed, "What? Did you just say what it sounded like you just said?"

"Yeah man, you heard right. Thai is ready to settle down. I want marriage. I want children. I want a more stable, secure life."

"Oh shit! What inspired this change of heart and mind?" Aaron asked.

"I've been thinking about this for a while, but what really did it was me driving down Michigan Ave and seeing a few things like…"

Aaron interrupted, "Like what?"

"Like a newly married couple kissing in their limo, and a father walking with his daughter on top of his shoulders. I want that, I need that."

Aaron sighed, "Man I thought I'd never live to see the day. I'm not lying to you."

Thailand shook his head, "Yeah me neither man, me neither…plus I saw the most beautiful woman that I've

EVER seen in my life walking past my business not too long ago!"

Aaron burst out laughing.

"I have never heard you say 'The most beautiful' nothing in my life! Did you talk to her?"

Thailand shook his head again, "Nope, but I have to find her…I have to."

Chapter Four

I am who I am

After kicking it on the phone with Thailand for about an hour, Aaron hung up and reflected on their conversation. Damn, Thai wants to settle down. I thought he would never come to his senses. Aaron thought about how he and Thailand had many arguments about Thai's 'free spirited' lifestyle. Aaron shook his head at the outcome of those verbal disputes. Speaking aloud, he said, "Thai always says that I'm judgmental, and think my way of life is the right way."

Aaron frowned, "When did I become like that bastard father of mine?"

Having a 'Five-star general officer for a father was extremely difficult for Aaron. He was never talked to, nor praised. All his father ever did was condemn and judge; he never showed love. Aaron was punished for showing any emotion that his father considered 'weak'. Nothing Aaron did was good enough. His father made sure that he embedded in his son's head that anything less than perfect would not be tolerated. He cut all ties to Aaron once Aaron told him that his dream was to own a restaurant one day. His father's last words echoed in his head…

    'You continue to be a disappointment to me boy. What real man wants to cook for a living? I said it then, and I'm going to say it again; I should have gotten a DNA test a long time ago, because there is no way someone like YOU was created by someone like ME.' Although those words were spoken almost ten years ago, they were still hard for Aaron to digest. He hadn't heard from his father since then, and Aaron couldn't care less.

Fuck that chump, Aaron thought. Any man that measures another man's worth based off of his goals, obviously has insecurities with himself. Aaron glanced around his home office and was quickly reminded of his loneliness.

"Shit, if Thai gets married before me, I'll never hear the end of it." He said leaning back in his chair.

"I hope this poetry set I'm debuting this Tuesday is a success. I might even spit something myself." Laughing out loud, he continued, "Thai is going to trip out because he hasn't heard me do spoken word since high school; back when we used to ditch last period and freestyle on different corners in the hood."

Thailand was really like the brother that he never had. They did everything together. They played the same sports, ate the same kind of foods, and liked the same girls. Aaron's smile quickly faded when his father tried to creep back into his mind. He quickly closed that door and began following up with the artists that were lined up for the poetry set. "All I know is that fool better remain in good health, because if he doesn't, father or not, he's going to be shit out of luck fucking with me." Aaron said to himself.

Chapter Five

Pimp down

Brooklyn pulled up to Derricka's condo and called her up.

"Hey girl I'm outside, and hurry up! I want to get a good table."

I promise you, I'll be sitting out here for about twenty minutes. This girl is such a slow poke, Brooklyn thought to herself. After about ten minutes, Derricka finally came outside. Twisting her face, she said, "Don't look at me like that! You know I have to get sexy."

Laughing Brooklyn said, "Get your ass in the car and let's go!"

Downtown Chicago was always over flowing with impatient taxi drivers, joggers, fast walking business men and women, and a line of luxury cars.

"I can't believe it took us 15 minutes to find a place to park!" Brooklyn said before slamming her car door.

"G, calm down. We're going to have a good time tonight, right?" Derricka stared at BK until she responded.

Rolling her eyes Brooklyn mumbled, "Yea right." Derricka smiled,

"Thank you, now let's find this joint."

Derricka walked into Aaron's, stunned by its romantic decor.

"BK you weren't lying, this place is beautiful!"

"I told you you'd like it."

Aaron's was full of conversation and laughter with smooth jazz playing in the background. To both women's satisfaction, they got a table close to the stage.

"Derri I can see myself being a regular here." Brooklyn looked up at Derricka to find her staring across the room.

"Derricka!"

Almost knocking her purse off the table, Derricka leaned over.

"BK do you see that man standing by the entrance door, wearing all black talking to the bus boy?"

Brooklyn looked over.

"Yea that's Aaron."

Derricka sighed, "Oh my God! BK he's coming over here." Aaron was in the midst of praising his staff for keeping things running smoothly, when he looked in Derricka's direction. Tapping his waiter Mike's shoulder, Aaron pointed.

"Mike look over there at the second table by the stage. Have you ever seen her in here before?"

Mike shook his head.

"Nope, I don't think so boss."

Aaron fixed his tie, "I didn't think so. I'd remember that face."

Aaron headed to the girls' table.

"Oh my goodness, Brooklyn he's gorgeous."

Brooklyn laughed, "Yes he is. I was on that lame ass date so I didn't try to holla."

All Aaron could think while walking over there was how beautiful Derricka was. She's so chocolate and voluptuous, he thought. Taking a deep breath, he approached the table.

"Hello ladies. Welcome to Aaron's. I'm Aaron, the..."

Brooklyn cut him off.

"You're Aaron, the owner, I know."

Aaron squinted his eyes.

"You're the woman that turned my place upside down the other night. How are you?" Aaron extended his hand to Brooklyn.

"I'm so sorry Aaron, I didn't mean to cause a scene at your place of business. I was just caught off guard by dude's ignorance; oh I'm Brooklyn by the way."

Aaron looked over at Derricka and reached for her hand.

"And you are?"

Derricka placed her hand in his, "I'm Derricka."

Aaron smiled, "Derricka...that's a beautiful name."

Derricka softly cleared her throat, "Thank you Aaron."

Brooklyn looked from Derricka to Aaron and then broke the awkward silence.

"So yeah, we would like a bottle of Barefoot Moscato."

"Oh yes, of course. I'll bring that right away."

Aaron released Derricka's hand, turning around only to bump into the neighboring table.

Brooklyn laughed, "Damn Derri! He's about to bust his shit looking at you."

Derricka just shook her head. Aaron sped towards the kitchen, this time bumping into his homeboy.

"Damn slow down gym shoe!" Thailand said while grabbing Aaron's arm.

"Hey Thai! Glad you could make it man. Walk to the back with me."

It took about a good five minutes for Aaron and Thailand to maneuver through the crowded restaurant.

"Damn man I didn't know your place get it cracking like this!"

Aaron laughed, "I swear to you, this has never happened before. All of these people... I'm happy and shocked." He looked back at Thailand, "Thai, what the hell are you grinning so hard for?"

"Okay, okay, okay, so check it. I sort of kind of felt bad about this being my first time coming to your place, so I had clients bring some people with them tonight."

Aaron cocked his head to the left, "Dude, are you serious?" Thailand nodded his head.

"Oh shit, so the majority of the new faces here tonight are your clients and friends of theirs?"

Thailand nodded again.

"Well damn. Now I see how you got that Benz." Aaron said.

Thailand burst out laughing.

"Like I said before, you know how I do."

They both headed out the kitchen door, when Aaron stopped and spun around.

"Ron, nigga what's wrong with you?!"

Aaron looked over his shoulder.

"Aye Thai, you see those two women sitting at the second table by the stage?

Thailand looked over, "Yea I see them, who's that, damn?!"

Aaron frowned, "They aren't clients of yours?"

"Hell no! I wish!"

Aaron rubbed his hands together.

"Good because I want the chocolate one."

Thailand raised his eyebrows.

"Oh no offense Thai, but I don't want your leftovers…that's why I asked."

"Whatever dude." said Thailand.

Aaron laughed, "I have a spot reserved up front for us by the stage. I plan on reading a piece, maybe two."

"Oh shit! I haven't heard you spit in a minute!" Thai said.

Aaron walked with Thai to table one and handed him a bottle of Moscato.

"Damn Aaron, can we have our bottle too?" Brooklyn shouted.

Derricka giggled at the look on Aaron's face.

"Brooklyn don't start tonight."

Brooklyn batted her eyes, "I'm going to be on my best behavior, promise."

Aaron looked at Derricka, "I'm sorry that I took so long." He said.

"No problem Aaron. I can see that you are quite busy tonight, anything special happening?"

Aaron smiled, "As a matter of fact it is. I'm having my very first poetry set tonight."

Brooklyn dropped her head.

"Really?! Brooklyn is a spoken word artist." Turning to her best friend, "BK you should hit the mic tonight."

Aaron shoved Brooklyn in the arm.

"You owe me anyway for turning my restaurant into a live soap opera. Besides, that will give me another reason to push my homey onto the stage."

They all laughed. Head in hands, Brooklyn agreed.

"I'll be sitting right here with my homeboy enjoying your performance." Aaron said while pointing back at Thailand. Not to Aaron's surprise, Thailand was macking some chicks at a neighboring table. Aaron shook his head, took the ladies' orders, and told them to enjoy the show that was scheduled to begin at 9:30 pm.

Brooklyn tapped Derricka's hand, "Looks like you've found a man."

"Please girl. Why do you say that?" asked Derricka

"Because from the look in your eyes, it looks like love at first sight."

Derricka rolled her eyes. She had forgotten all about her best friend being a hopeless romantic. You could never tell at first but underneath the tough exterior, Brooklyn was as soft as cotton. The vibe inside Aaron's was so serene. The band played old tunes from Ella Fitzgerald to Coltrane. The food was delicious. Both women ordered fish dishes, and were halfway through the bottle of wine, when the lights dimmed and Aaron walked on stage.

"Hello ladies and gentlemen. Thank you for coming out to my place tonight. I'm Aaron and I have something special to give to you."

He closed his eyes, took a deep breath, and grabbed the mic.

"Such a beautiful sadness

The rise of a black Sun

I have come undone

In the heart of this madness

Don't scorn me Black one

Songs of secrets~ my heart has sung

In the midst of it all, I'm passing

Tell my father that I love him~ but my thoughts are
crashing

So he might not know me anymore

I

Am

Poetry's whore

I have to write to survive

You~ black one

Have sparked flames in my eyes

So to sorrow I gotta say~ good bye

Because I'm stronger now

I feel empowered now

My soul was cracked into pieces

It hurt

That my hands couldn't catch all the pieces

But that's over now

Because I know what peace is

Such a beautiful sadness

The rise of a black Sun~ has saved me from me

How I am now

Is who I will be

How I was then~ of that now

I am free."

 Aaron opened his eyes, startled at the round of applause that echoed in the room.

"Thank you. Thank you so much." Waving his hands for spectators to sit back in their seats and quiet down, Aaron spoke.

"Tonight's poetic theme is life. If you poets are bold enough, you all will share with us your life, allowing us to get a better understanding of who you are. So without further ado, I would like to bring up a poet that goes by the name of 'Luscious'. Give it up for Ms. Luscious!" Aaron exited the stage and sat next to Thailand.

"Good piece Ron Ron. I see you still spit that fire."

Aaron rubbed his head, "Shit man I was nervous as hell! That's why I had my eyes closed the entire time." Aaron did a double take when he looked at the stage.

"Damn Thai, she popped! She looks like Curious George with a blonde weave, damn!"

Thailand glanced at the stage and spit out his moscato, "Lauryn!"

Thailand's secretary was standing on stage in gold go-go boots, an orange mini skirt, and a peach tank top; looking as if a toddler did her make-up.

"Hi my name is Luscious and I would like to dedicate this piece to Mr. Thailand Moore here."

Thailand and Aaron's eyes widened.

"Thai baby, nobody, and I mean nobody does my body like you do. I just want everybody to know that all this is yours. Any…….time…….you want it." Licking her lips, she wrapped both hands around the microphone.

"We fuck so pretty

Drink me~ how do I taste?

How many licks does it take

For me to rain down on your face?

Mmm….mmm good!

Campbell's soup ain't got shit on me

You're right where you're supposed to be

Resting between my knees

I'm not satisfied yet

I wanna get drunk off your sex

I wanna overdose on orgasm

I want to cum harder than before

I'm your personal whore

So bang me until I'm sore

Anything you give~ I'll always want more

Because you're so good

So good

So muthafucking good

For my soul and body

My ears thumping with Prince 'Erotic City'

That song describes us perfectly

I look into your eyes and mouth the words

We fuck so pretty."

Aaron stood up and burst out laughing and clapping. Thailand just stared at the stage with his mouth wide open.

"Thai baby, close your mouth, before I sit this pussy in it." Lauryn said before exiting the stage.

Aaron was leaning over the table laughing with tears in his eyes.

"Aaron man, this shit isn't funny. Look around the room. These women are pissed!"

Aaron wiped his eyes and glanced around the room. Damn near everyone was scowling at Thailand and shaking their heads.

"Damn man, you might want to go see if your tires are sliced or some shit." Aaron said.

Thailand rested his head on the table. Aaron looked over at Derricka and Brooklyn.

"Aye you, Brooklyn, it's your turn."

Brooklyn frowned, "Fuck that! I'm not going up after that craziness."

Aaron felt a tap on his shoulder.

"Excuse me sir, I know I didn't sign up, but do you mind if I step to the mic?"

Aaron turned around to see a woman who had the biggest green eyes he'd ever seen. She was medium height, shoulder length brown hair with funky angles, with a petite shape. Thailand lifted his head to see the woman he'd been thinking about for the past couple of days.

"Aaron, it's her."

Looking back at Thailand, "This is the woman you've been thinking about none stop?" Aaron asked.

Thailand nodded his head.

"Excuse me. I'm sorry, do I know you?" she asked.

Thailand just stared.

"So it's Mr. Aaron, right? Can I get on the mic?"

"Of course Ms. Lady, go right ahead."

Nodding, she walked on stage and took the mic off the stand.

"My name is Adriana, and I would like to share a piece that I wrote not too long ago. Since we're talking about our lives, I feel this will be the appropriate place and time to express these feelings I have." Tucking her hair behind her left ear, she began.

"Raggedy

Bitch ass

Soft

Mama boys

No sense having

4 inch dicks

Oogly faces

Lazy~ whack ass lovers

No aspirations

No goals

No drive

No desire to do shit

Still living at home

Don't think their shit stank ass men!

I'm tired

I'm so tired of being your mother

Your wife

Your lover

Your accountant

Your common sense

Your psychiatrist

Your best friend

Your cook

Your massage therapist

Only to be mistreated~ misused

Unappreciated

Fucked over

Forgotten

Number 10 on your 'To do list'

When I should be number 1 because I have pussy remember?

Silly tired ass

Humping like a dog in heat

Because they have no idea how to make love

Low- self esteem

Cry baby ass

Content with living paycheck to paycheck

Want to be considered a 'Man'

But only know 'Lucifer' as a Jay-Z song

And not another name for the devil

Dumb ass men.

I'm tired

I'm sick of these 45 second men

I'm tired

So sick of these 'I want to have a baby with you'

But don't' take care of the 5 kids they already have ass men

Don't matter the age or race

These men are just raggedy nowadays."

All the women stood up and clapped. Brooklyn was the first one to shoot out of her seat.

"You damn right Adriana. YOU DAMN RIGHT! Raggedy ass bastards! Tell 'em girl!" yelled Brooklyn. Adriana left the stage smiling.

"Thanks Aaron for letting me crash your poetry set. I appreciate it."

Aaron extended his hand.

"Oh no problem, you were damn good. I'd love to have you as a regular."

"Yea we'd love to have you as a regular." Thailand said grabbing her hand.

"Hi I'm Thailand, and I was very moved by your poem. I saw you walk pass my spa the other day, and I haven't been able to get you off my mind"

Aaron rolled his eyes.

"Thank you Thailand. And by the way, I love your name." Thailand smiled. "

"Thank you. So are you from here?"

But before Adrianna could answer, Lauryn interrupted.

"Um excuse me, but Thailand is spoken for."

"By whom?" Thailand asked.

"By me, didn't you feel anything from the poem I wrote about us?"

Thailand grabbed Lauryn's hand.

"Excuse us Adriana, I'll be right back. Don't leave okay?"

"That bitch can leave!" Lauryn shouted.

"I'll be right here." Adriana replied giggling. Thailand dragged Lauryn to the kitchen. Spinning her around.

"What the fuck is wrong with you Lauryn?!"

"No Thai, what the fuck is wrong with you?! You telling me I've just been an object to you all of these months?! Just a fucking toy?! Huh Thai?! All these bitches in here you've fucked and now the bitch that strolled past the office is going to be your new dip?! Shit Thailand I love you! I want you! I've given you every part of me and you're acting like you don't feel the same!"

"Because I don't! It was just sex. I've never held you after. I've never kissed you. I've never laid up with you after we were done. I've never called you just to hang out. I've never held your hand or caressed you. What we did was pure fucking, that's it! Now get your crazy ass out of this restaurant and please don't think for one goddamn second that you still have a job, because you would be sadly mistaken."

Lauryn unexpectedly grabbed a chef's knife and lunged at Thailand, making him knock over trays of food. Thailand tried to grab Lauryn, but she managed to cut the palm of his right hand.

"Bitch what the fuck is wrong with you?! Put the knife down!"

"No nigga, if I can't have you, none of these chickens will!"

Lauryn lunged at Thailand again, this time knocking cloth napkins onto an open fire. After two more cuts on the arm and elbow, Thailand wrestled Lauryn to the floor as the smoke detector rang out.

"Let me go! Let me go before I press charges! You're hurting me Thailand!"

Aaron burst through the kitchen doors.

"What the hell is going on?!"

Choking from the smoke, Aaron grabbed Thailand by the arm.

"Thai, come on man we have to get out of here, now!" Thailand lifted Lauryn off the ground, twisted her arms back and pushed her out of the kitchen.

"Ouch! Thai, you are going to break my arm."

"That would be good for your psycho ass." Thailand said through clinched teeth. The fire spread quickly and people were hunched over coughing from the smoke.

"Everybody out! Get outside!" Aaron yelled as he began guiding people out the door.

Someone called 911, because firemen were coming in as people were scrambling out. Aaron saw Derricka kneeling on the floor.

"Derricka, come on!"

"I can't! Brooklyn's not breathing! I can't leave my best friend." Aaron ran over to her side, but was moved out of the way by a fireman.

"You two need to get out now. I'll take care of her." said the fireman.

Aaron grabbed Derricka's hand and they both rushed out of the restaurant.

Chapter Six

Chaos

The fireman scooped Brooklyn up and maneuvered his way through the smoke to the outside.

"Everybody move back! Give me some room."

He laid Brooklyn on the ground and checked for a pulse.

"Shit she's not breathing!"

He began performing CPR on Brooklyn, but after three sets of two breaths, and thirty chest compressions, Brooklyn still wasn't responding. Damn, I never had to go all the way to five sets before. They usually wake up by now, he thought to himself. Derricka saw the concern on the fireman's face and pushed past a spectator.

"What the fuck are you doing wrong that she's not responding?!" screamed Derricka.

The fireman shot her a 'Shut the fuck up' look then gave Brooklyn two breaths.

"C'mon lady breathe." He mumbled.

He was about to give her two more breaths when Brooklyn coughed.

"Oh my God! Brooklyn!" Derricka cried.

"Ma'am are you alright?" the fireman asked.

Brooklyn stared at Ethan before answering.

"Yes. What happened?"

"There was a fire in the restaurant and you passed out from the smoke." Ethan explained.

Brooklyn touched his shoulder with tears in her eyes.

"Thank you so much for saving me. I don't remember seeing smoke. Is everyone alright Mr...?"

"Ethan. My name is Ethan."

"Well thank you Ethan."

"I can't believe the paramedics are just getting here." Ethan said, looking over his shoulder.

Brooklyn stood up when a paramedic approached her.

"Who the fuck are you all coming to save?! I have visited the Lord and came back fucking with y'all?!" Brooklyn screamed.

Ethan burst out laughing.

"Ma'am can we please check you out, put you on some oxygen and make sure there are no head injuries from you fainting?"

"Get the fuck out of my face. Where is Derricka?" Brooklyn looked by the ambulance to see Thailand getting treated by a paramedic while in handcuffs. Aaron was talking to officers, and Derricka was sitting on the curb crying.

"Derri what's wrong with you? I'm alive, see?" Derricka reached up and hugged Brooklyn.

"I'm such a bad friend. I didn't want to leave you, but they made me."

"Derri pull yourself together! That fireman told you right. You could've passed out with me."

Brooklyn broke the embrace.

"Please tell me you got Aaron's number?"

Derricka laughed.

"Yea he gave me his card before all this went down."

"Cool. Now let's get out of here so you can tell me what the hell happened."

The paramedics finally convinced Brooklyn to get checked over, after one last tongue lashing.

****

"Officer she's lying. My friend was defending himself. You see, he's the one that's getting stitched up not her!" Aaron said pointing at Lauryn.

Scratching his disgustingly oversized belly, the officer pointed at Thailand.

"He doesn't look that hurt to me. Listen it's her word against his and you walked in on the end of it, so you don't really know what happened yourself."

Aaron dropped his head. Thailand was being put in the squad car when Lauryn ran up and smacked the officer.

"I love him! Let him go! How are we supposed to be together if he's locked up?!"

The officer stopped talking to Aaron and ran over to subdue Lauryn.

"See! See what I'm saying? She's crazy!" Thailand yelled as he was shoved in the back seat of a squad car.

"Aaron I'm sorry!" Thailand said.

"Yea me too." Aaron replied as the squad car drove off.

Chapter Seven

I'm a hustler

Ethan was being teased all week at the fire station for saving Brooklyn.

"Man I'm not being mean but, I wouldn't have kept going. My arms get tired quickly." One fireman said.

Ethan looked at him. "You're bogus for that Chris."

"Oh I'm bogus because I wouldn't have kept kissing her and touching her chest? Riiggght."

"I was trying to save her, not freak her, dumb ass." All of the firemen laughed simultaneously. Stuffing a donut in his mouth, Chris threw up his hands.

"Well excuuse me! Don't hit me!"

"Whatever dude." Ethan said walking out the station.

Fuck, I want to relax but I have to train for my upcoming fight, Ethan thought. He was not only a part time Chicago fireman, but he was a well-known boxer as well. Ethan had to learn how to fight at an early age if he wanted to survive the streets of the Westside of Chicago. When he was 11 years old, his mother kicked him out of the house for looking too much like his father. Ethan did everything from stealing food and cars, to selling drugs just to eat. He slept in crack houses and under different viaducts almost every night. Other nights he'd roam the streets looking for something to get into. One night he walked up on a street brawl and stood watching in fascination. People were cheering the fighters on as they waved money in the air. Wow you can make money street brawling? Young Ethan thought. That night inspired him to fight to survive, not steal, and sell dope. Ethan mimicked the moves of the fighters that he watched every night…until he was 16 years old; that's when he was set up to be robbed and murdered.

Chapter Eight

It's a hard knock life

Adriana couldn't believe that she jumped on stage at Aaron's like that.

"I can't believe I let my ex get me so emotional that I wrote a poem about him, AND THEN performed it!" Adriana said to herself.

She thought about how that Thailand guy had asked her to wait for him, but he was taking too long, so she bounced. "I'm glad that I did." she said aloud.

Adriana pondered on the fire and how, with her luck, she would have been a victim. Her life had been nothing but 'bad breaks' since she could remember. She was told that her mother was Jamaican and her father was white. Her mother was young when she had her, and her father didn't want it to be known that he was with a black woman. Adriana's mother left her in a crate on top of a garbage can in a random alley. The following morning, two garbage men found her and took her to the nearest hospital. From there on, Adriana bounced from foster home to foster home. She lived on the streets after running away from foster parents, who either tried to molest her or beat her. She never had a best friend or a boyfriend, because she never cared to become emotionally attached to anyone. The closest person she had to a friend was a homeless thug that fought all the time, and his name was Ethan. She taught him a few things on how to survive in the streets. She first met him when they were both around 11 years old. He was going through the garbage looking for food.

"Hey boy! The church on Austin right off division is giving away soup and bread. Go get you some before they run out." said Adriana.

Running past Adriana, Ethan yelled, "Thank you!"

"You're welcome." she said under breath, "Damn he's running fast as hell."

She watched Ethan sprint to the church.

****

"Adriana we're ready to begin our lesson." A lady said.

Adriana snapped out of thought, "Tara I'm sorry! Let's begin."

Adriana teaches art class to emotionally disabled adults whose tempers made them hazardous to themselves and to others. They were people who had been drugged for depression, and other normal things human beings go through. She teaches them that they aren't disturbed, but are sensitive to life, and that they can grow tougher skin if they learned to get back up when life knocked them down. She teaches them how to move on. Adriana turned to her students and explained the lesson for the day.

"Now everyone in this room is over 25, so I know you have a story to tell. I want you to take your most vivid memory, either pleasant or not, and paint it." Adriana said.

Reaching behind her canvas, she grabbed her iPod and turned on 'Slow Down' by Flying Lotus.

"Adriana, are you joining us in the lesson?" asked one of her students

Adriana smiled, "Yes I am, and it's long overdue." Adriana turned up the volume and took a deep breath.

Chapter Nine

Mommy's Whore

After 10 hours of interrogation, Lauryn finally broke down and told the truth about how the fire started. The big bellied policeman from the scene walked into the room where Thailand was being held, and told him the good news.

"You got lucky son. She confessed. You have two options, and I will advise that you take the second one. You can walk out of here and forget the whole thing, or you can press charges and get a restraining order against her fatal attraction having ass; so what's it gonna be?"

"I'm most definitely pressing charges." said Thailand.

"Smart brain you got there, son. C'mon so we can get this over and done with."

It took Thailand about another hour to fill out paper work before he left the station.

Aaron was sitting in his car when he saw Thailand walking down the stairs of the police station.

"Thai! Over here!" Aaron yelled out the window. Thailand jogged over to the car and got in.

"Aaron man what are you doing here?" Thailand asked.

"What the fuck you mean? I shouldn't be?" Aaron asked frowning.

"No it's just…it's just I thought you'd be pissed at me for what happened. I swear to the Lord I'll pay what I can to get your spot back in shape." said Thailand.

"I have insurance on the place. I'm meeting the people later on today, and hopefully renovations will start next week. But I am pissed at that bitch for trying to put my bro in the dirt. I hope you are done sleeping around. This is a lesson to treasure, not toss Thai."

Thai reclined his seat, "I know man. I'm a one woman man from here on out."

Aaron laughed, "Shit I hope your word is bond. And I meant to tell you…that Adriana chick looked good!"

"I told you man. When she walked past my place I couldn't take my eyes off of her. We didn't exchange numbers or shit, so that's down the drain."

Aaron shook his head, "You never know. You just never know."

On the ride to Thailand's house, he told Aaron about Lauryn's confession and the restraining order.

"Man I have to change all of the locks to the spa and my crib. This is some bull." Thailand said.

"Yep, sounds like a good idea to me bro." Aaron said.

Thailand gave Aaron daps and hopped out of the car. He grabbed the mail and walked into his 3 bedroom house, exhausted from the previous events. Resting in his recliner, he rustled through his mail.

"Bill. Bill. Bill. All these fucking bills!"

Sitting up in his chair, he stared at a letter. What the fuck is Sahara writing me for? He thought. He never called her mom or mother, just her name, Sahara. Thailand despised her. The things she used to require him do makes him quiver. Ripping open the envelope, Thailand became angry.

"I'm not giving this bitch no money…not even a fucking kidney. Shit I was hoping she died already." he said aloud.

Dear Son,

I am sending this letter to inform you that I am dying. I have cancer and the doctors say I'm too far along for treatment, so I felt it was only right to make peace with you. I know I was a horrible mother. Sometimes I wonder why you were never taken away from me for the things I subjected you to. Son I'm so sorry for allowing the drugs and the alcohol to take priority in my life. Everything that happened, I swear I was high or drunk. I was not sober. If I could take it back, I would never have let those women.....

Thailand folded up the letter and tossed it onto the coffee table. Fuck that bitch, Thailand thought as he stripped off his clothes, walking to the bathroom.

"Damn this water feels good." Leaning against the shower door, he shook his head, "What the fuck does Sahara think is going to happen? I'm supposed to say mama I forgive you? I'll be here for you until your last days? Bitch please."

Sahara got so deep into drugs that she started prostituting Thailand to pay for her daily fixes. The first time was when he was 7 years old. He was sitting in his room counting how many roaches climbed the wall when his mother called his name.

"Thailand come here! I would like for you to meet someone!"

Rolling his eyes, Thailand went into the front room where he saw his mother sitting with a lady that he'd never saw before. The lady was pale white, with smeared hot pink lipstick, crust in the corners of her mouth, and was extremely thin.

"Thailand baby, meet Ms. Candice."

Candice leaned over and stroked his face.

"You are such a handsome dark thing."

Sahara moved Candice's hand away.

"Uh uhn, no touching until the money is in my hands. So, where is it?"

Candice reached into her bra and pulled out a $20 bill. Grinning like a child getting their favorite candy, Sahara snatched the bill and pulled Thailand close.

"Listen baby, I need you to show mama how much you love her and how much of a big boy you are, okay?

Now I want you to do what Ms. Candice tells you to, alright?"

Thailand said okay and walked with Candice to his mother's bedroom. Closing the door behind them, Candice pointed to Thailand's pants and told him to take them off.

"But why do I have to take my pants off? It's cold in here. There's no heat in the house."

Candice reached back and smacked Thai.

"Do like I said!

Crying, Thailand unbuckled his pants and let them drop to the floor. Candice pulled down his underwear.

"I see you are going to be blessed down there when you get older, and I will most definitely be back to get some of that. Now take my pants off."

Thailand did as he was told, and started undressing her. Wherever she told him to touch or kiss, he did. These sessions with her, and many other women would continue until he was 15. Thailand stepped out of the shower and wiped the steam from the mirror with his hand and said, "And that was the birth of Thailand the player."

Chapter Ten

Love at 1st & 2nd sight

Derricka held her cell phone in one hand, and Aaron's card in the other.

"BK, do you really think I should call after all that's happened? I mean he might not be in good spirits right now."

Brooklyn snatched Derricka's phone and the card.

"Fuck it! I'll call him, because you're tripping Derricka." Laughing, Derricka snatched her phone back and popped Brooklyn on the arm.

"Shut up! I'm about to call him. Give me the card."

Derricka dialed the numbers and looked at Brooklyn before she pressed the send button.

"Girl stop being so dramatic and call the man." said Brooklyn.

****

Aaron was on the phone talking to Thailand about his mother's letter when his other line beeped.

"Man Thai that's crazy as hell. What makes her think that shit will be peaches and cream because she's dying? Aye hold on, someone's on the other end."

Aaron clicked over, "Hello this is Aaron."

"Hi, this is Derricka."

Aaron paused, "I didn't think you would ever call, how are you doing?"

"I'm good. I'm so sorry about your restaurant. What's the status on that?" Derricka asked.

"It's looking up, but hold on, let me hang up with Thailand."

Aaron clicked back over.

"Aye Thai, let me hit you back, Derricka's on the other line."

"What?! That chocolate thing you were drooling over?" Thailand said laughingly.

"Dude please! The same way you were drooling over Adriana, remember that?"

"Man whatever, just call me back."

"Yeah alright." Aaron agreed.

"Derricka?"

"Yea I'm still here. Umm, Aaron, I was wondering if we could have dinner sometime."

Damn she beat me to it, he thought.

"Yea I would like that, how about tonight?"

"Tonight is good, around seven-ish?" Derricka suggested.

"Seven-ish sounds good."

The two decided to eat at the Grand Lux Café, and to take a stroll along the lakefront. Derricka gave Aaron her home address before they said their goodbyes. She hung up the phone with a huge smile on her face.

"Girl you act like you never went on a date before." Brooklyn said frowning.

"Shut up BK! I'm excited! He seems like a decent guy."

Brooklyn rolled her eyes. "Just don't bump uglies with him tonight... it's un-lady like."

Laughing, Derricka opened the door to her closet.

"Whatever okay? Just help me find something to wear."

Aaron hung with Derricka and immediately called Thailand back.

"So Derricka and I are having dinner tonight at the Grand Lux."

"Oh word? That's a romantic joint like your place. They have good food, but their tables by the windows are extra small." Warned Thailand.

"Who did you take there, Lauryn?" Aaron said laughingly."

"Ahahaha, not funny at all, and no I didn't."

"If you say so, let me get off this phone and wrap up this paper work. It's already 4:45." said Aaron.

"Cool just let me know how it goes tonight. I'll holla." Thailand said.

Brooklyn set Derricka's shoes next to the dress and accessories that she picked out for the date.

"Derri, I laid everything out on the bed, I have to ride, I have to get ready myself." said Brooklyn.

"Where the hell are you going?" Derricka stuck her head out the bathroom.

"I'm meeting a co-worker at Bar Louie's for a few drinks, nosy ass!" answered Brooklyn.

"Alright well I'll text you to let you know how the date is going. If he's whack as hell, I might come to Bar Louie's!" said Derricka.

Brooklyn laughed, "I doubt that. Aaron seems like a cool guy."

We will see, thought Derricka.

****

A few hours after leaving Derricka's, Brooklyn was sitting at a table explaining how she almost died in the fire at Aaron's.

"Lana I'm telling you, I saw the white light."

Lana took a long sip of her margarita, "I'm just glad you're okay. The school in general thrives off teachers like you." Lana continued, "If I were you, I would have sent that fireman a card or something, because he could have given up on you."

Brooklyn bopped her head in agreement.

"Yea he could have given up, but he didn't, and I'm beyond grateful." she said.

Lana cleared her throat, "Let's change the topic to a happier one. So was he cute?"

Brooklyn choked on her drink, "Was who cute, the fireman?"

"Yea who else?!" said Lana.

"Oh yeah, he is handsome. He's brown skinned with dark brown eyes, with a dimple in his left cheek."

Lana threw back the last of her margarita.

"Shit that sounds good to me. I hope you see him again."

"Yeah me too Lana. I don't think I could thank him enough."

****

Derricka was putting on her make-up when Aaron called.

"Hey you, I'm almost ready."

"Good, because I'm pulling up on your block." he said.

"Okay I'll be out in a minute."

Derricka grabbed her purse and headed out the door.

"Wow, you look beautiful."

Derricka smiled,"Why thank you Aaron."

Aaron opened the passenger door, and before he could open his, she reached over and popped his lock.

"It's funny you did that."

Derricka laughed, "And why is that?"

"Because I just watched a movie called 'A Bronx Tale' with Robert Deniro."

"Oh yeah I know what you're talking about, when Sonny told Calogero that the way to tell if Jane was the right one, was if she opened the door for him after she got in the car." Derricka continued," I love that movie."

"I do too."

They discussed all of their favorite movies and actors and in no time, they were at the restaurant. The valet took Aaron's car as he and Derricka entered the Grand Lux Cafe.

"Thai was right. This place has a romantic feel like mines."

"Hello! Welcome to the Grand Lux Café, A table for two?" asked the matradee.

"Yes, just two, and can we have a booth please?" Aaron asked.

"How did you know that I prefer booths over tables?" asked Derricka.

"Lucky guess." Aaron said with a smile.

They ordered and drank white wine while continuing their conversation from the car. They both exchanged thoughts on food, wine, music, and their professions.

"Wow, I've never met a live artist before. Hopefully one day I will become your muse." said Aaron.

Derricka laughed, "Only time will tell Aaron."

The food and the service were satisfactory, so they left their waiter a nice tip.

"Wow! Thanks guys! You two have a wonderful evening." said the waiter.

"Are you ready to walk the lake?" Aaron said as he grabbed Derricka's hand.

Derricka nodded her head, and they drove to the lakefront.

Brooklyn and Lana were laughing at how Brooklyn cursed out Jayden's mom, when she saw Ethan walk into the bar.

"Lana you won't believe me if I tell you this." said Brooklyn.

"Tell me what?"

"You know the fireman that saved my life?"

Lana nodded.

"Girl that's him by the bar with the fitted white sox hat."

Lana eyes got big, "Damn! He's sexy as hell! Shit!" Lana tapped Brooklyn's hand, "Girl, go over there before these chickens swarm around him and ruin y'all hooking up." Brooklyn frowned, "Hooking up? Nobody said anything about hooking up with him."

"Brooklyn please go over there."

Brooklyn took a deep breath and walked over to Ethan.

"Hi Ethan."

Ethan looked out the corner of his eye, "Hey, how are you doing?"

"I'm good thanks to you. I don't think I ever told you my name, I'm Brooklyn."

Ethan smiled, "Brooklyn. That's unique."

"Thank you. Ethan I just wanted to thank you again, I really appreciate you.

Ethan shook his head, "I was just doing my job."

Brooklyn looked down at his bruised knuckles.

"Did you get into a fight?" she asked.

Ethan followed her eyes to his hands, "Well not technically; I was sparring. I'm also a boxer." Ethan replied.

"Really? I love boxing."

Ethan lifted his left brow, "You love boxing? You're into sports?"

"Psh! Hell to the yes! Boxing, UFC fighting, basketball, football, and tennis."

"That's what's up. Maybe you can come to my next match Wednesday night." said Ethan.

"I would love to. How can I get in touch with you?"

"Give me your number and I'll call your phone right now." Brooklyn told Ethan her number and got up to leave.

"Wait…do you want a drink or something?" Ethan asked.

"Could you order me an apple martini? I'm going to walk my friend out, be right back."

Ethan agreed and Brooklyn met Lana at the door.

"Lana, he has the most beautiful eyes! They are driving me crazy! You know that's my fetish."

"Look don't give him any nookie yet, and call me later. You know I'm nosy." Lana said laughingly.

Brooklyn waved goodbye to Lana and went back into the bar.

"I'm so sorry, was I gone too long?"

"Nope. So do you really have the nerve to watch me box? It's going to be bloody, I'm a monster in the ring." he warned.

"A monster, why are you a monster in the ring?"

Ethan took two shots of Ciroc to the head before answering.

"Fighting allows me to release all of my frustration and stress without going to jail."

They both laughed.

"Well that makes sense." said Brooklyn.

They talked about the two loves of their lives, teaching and boxing, until they were the last two in the bar.

"Wow it's almost 2 a.m. We should get going." Brooklyn said.

"Yeah, I'll drop you off."

Brooklyn stopped at the door.

"Wait, are you good to drive? You knocked back a couple of vodkas."

Ethan cocked his head, and Brooklyn threw up her hands.

"Aye I'm just saying. You put all that work in saving me I don't want that to be in vain."

Ethan laughed, "You are funny, let's go."

Ethan pulled up in front of Brooklyn's apartment.

"Brooklyn, I enjoyed conversing with you tonight. I hope we can do it again."

"I enjoyed myself too, and I wouldn't mind seeing you again. Call me and we'll set something up…walk me to my door?"

Chapter Eleven

New Beginnings

Brooklyn sent Derricka a text on the way home, but she never responded.

"Let me call this chick". She dialed her number and it went straight to voicemail. What the hell? Her phone is never off. I hope she's okay, thought Brooklyn. Brooklyn decided to wait an hour before she tried Derricka again. She was in the shower when her phone rang. "Shit that might be Derri." Brooklyn grabbed a towel and ran in her bedroom. She smiled when she saw that it was Ethan. Before they departed, she asked him to let her know when he made it home safely. Hmm, I like that. A grown man that listens, she thought.

"Hey, made it home safe?" she asked.

"Yes ma'am, but that's not the only reason I called." Brooklyn sat on the bed.

"Is there something wrong Ethan?"

"No, I just wanted to ask you, would you like to come to the gym and watch me train, and then maybe have dinner?" he asked.

"That sounds exciting. Sure I will come. Around what time?"

"Four p.m. at the YMCA in Oak park."

"No problem, I'll be there." replied Brooklyn.

"Cool, see you later on."

"Okay I'll see you tomorrow." Brooklyn hung up with a bittersweet feeling. On one hand, she was really feeling Ethan, and on the other, she was worried about Derricka. This was so unlike her to not call or text. I hope Aaron's being a gentlemen, I don't want to have to cut his ass, she thought. She dried off, said her prayers and called it a night.

"No worries, she'll call me later."

****

Derricka was awakened by the laughter of children and a cool breeze. She realized that she and Aaron had fallen asleep on a blanket, and that she was wrapped in his arms. Mmmm, he feels so good, Derricka thought as she snuggled her face into his chest. She managed to free her arm so she could trace his face with her fingers. Her index finger rested on his lips, when Aaron tilted her head back and kissed her. She placed her hand behind his head and kissed him deeper.

Derricka smiled against his lips, "Good afternoon Mr. Gentry."

Aaron kissed her again, "Good afternoon Ms. Fallon. I have a suggestion."

"And what's that?" Derricka asked.

"I suggest we go to my place and get cleaned up, have some lunch, and catch a movie."

"I like that suggestion a lot but umm, I don't have clothes at your place."

"Oh we can fix that. Let's go get you something to wear from somewhere in the area real quick."

The two had gathered their things and was headed to the car when Derricka turned to Aaron.

"Wait a minute, you're buying this outfit, correct?" Aaron burst out laughing, "Nah you're buying it, and everything else I want in life, now bring your ass!"

The first thought that came to Derricka's mind when she walked in Aaron's house was that it looked like Patricia's and Gavin's home from the movie, 'Why did I get married.'

"Aaron, your house looks beautiful. I love the colors and the art work." said Derricka.

"Thanks. The art work is by this painter named A.J. no one has ever seen or met A.J. Art collectors don't even know if A.J is a man or a woman. I've tried to google the hell out of this painter, but nothing comes up. Here, let me show you where to go." Aaron guided Derricka upstairs through the master bedroom into the master bathroom. He gave her towels and started the shower for her.

"When you're done, come down stairs and I'll start making lunch." he said.

"Aaron wait, will you undress me?"

Aaron stared at Derricka before he walked over to her.

"Only if I can get in with you."

He undressed and joined her behind the steamed glass.

He held her from behind and whispered in her ear, "Wash me first?"

Derricka squeezed some body wash into her hands and begin massaging his penis as she kissed his chest.

"Mmmm....shit bay." Aaron moaned.

Derricka dropped to her knees and started teasing him with her tongue. Hot and bothered, Aaron grabbed a handful of Derricka's hair and stood her up.

"You really want to do this?" he asked.

She whispered 'Yes' against his lips. He pushed her against the glass, wrapped one of her legs around his waist, put the other on his shoulder, and then penetrated her.

"Mmm....Aaron."

"Derricka open your eyes and look at me."

Derricka's eyes met Aaron's.

"I want you to see how good you feel to me."

Intensely staring into each other's eyes, they made love, frantically.

Aaron slid Derricka down and kisses her.

"I hope you don't think I'm a slut for sleeping with you on the second date. I'm really a good guy."

Derricka laughed, "Well you know I'm going tell my home girls how I got those drawers on the second date." she teased.

Aaron laughed and slid his hands in between Derricka's legs.

"Come on let's go eat lunch before I pin you against this glass again."

****

Brooklyn was amazed at Ethan's work ethic. He was very precise and sharp in his movements. All it took was two punches to the ribs, followed by an overhand right, to have his sparring partner hit the ground, knocked out.

"Ethan! What I tell you?! If you keep knocking out your sparring partners, THEY ARE NOT GONNA WANT TO SPAR ANY MORE! And I'm damn sure not getting in the ring with you." yelled Joe.

Ethan just stared at him.

"Okay, I didn't mean to raise my voice Ethan, but stop beating your sparring partners like they stole something; we need them to train with."

"Cut this tape off Joe." commanded Ethan.

Joe did as he was told, then mumbled, 'Sensitive ass boy' under his breath when Ethan walked over to Brooklyn.

"Wow Ethan, you looked great. I've never seen anyone so focused in my life."

"Thanks. Let me take a quick shower then we can head out."

"Okay I'll sit here and talk to Joe." Brooklyn said.

"I love talking to pretty women such as yourself." said Joe."

"Aye man, she's mine." Ethan said jogging backwards out of the gym.

Joe shook his head. "Like I said, sensitive ass boy." Brooklyn laughed.

■■

Derricka walked into Aaron's kitchen wearing the outfit he bought her.

"Damn Derricka! Those jeans are fitting you right!" Derricka giggled, "Mmmm it smells good in here, what are we eating?"

"We are eating grilled salmon, mixed veggies, rice and French bread."

"Damn Aaron! I came up in the world. I found a man that has good dick AND can cook. I'm a lucky gal."

Aaron burst out laughing. After they ate launch they went to see a new action flick that came out the week before.

"Derricka, I had a good time with you and I hope we can do this again soon."

Derricka wrapped her arms around his neck.

"We most definitely can do this again."

She stood on her tip toes to kiss him. They parted ways and agreed to meet up again in a few days. Derricka laid across her bed on cloud nine. She had never felt so good before.

"Shit I have three photo shoots tomorrow! Let me hit the sack."

****

Brooklyn and Ethan were having dinner at the 'Volare' when Ethan noticed Brooklyn was being really quiet.

"What's up Bay? What's on your mind?" Ethan inquired.

"You remember my best friend that was yelling at you when you were giving me CPR? Well I haven't talked to her since yesterday evening; I was helping her get ready for a date."

Ethan took a bite of his food.

"So maybe she spent the night with him, and her phone's dead."

Brooklyn shook her head, "That's not Derricka at all, which is why I'm worried."

"If it's bothering you that much, we can swing by her place when we're done."

Brooklyn agreed and about an hour later she was ringing her best friend's doorbell. Derricka jumped out of bed livid.

"Who the fuck is ringing my doorbell like they are stupid?!" Derricka spoke through the intercom, "Who the fuck is it?"

"It's me, Brooklyn. Let me in."

Derricka buzzed Brooklyn up to her apartment.

"BK, what are you doing here?" Derricka questioned.

"Derri, I've been texting and calling you since last night, and you never answered. I thought Aaron did something to you."

"He did. He gave me some good dick. Plus I'm just getting home from being with him a little while ago." Brooklyn took a step back and folded her arms.

"So you're telling me that you had not one moment to call or text that you were alright Derricka?"

"Brooklyn I didn't think about it. What the hell is the problem?" Derricka wanted to know.

"The problem is…you left your best friend worried that your body was in the damn river, because you went on a date with a man that you just met." Brooklyn replied.

"BK let's get something straight. I'm a grown ass woman, and I don't have to report or check in with you. I've been grown for a long time and my mother walked out on me and my sisters, so I don't answer to NO female. The quicker you understand that, the better."

Brooklyn nodded her head, "Well understand this Derricka, you got this female right here fucked up, and I put it on my life, that you will never have to worry about none of this shit again…and word is bond." Brooklyn stormed out of Derricka's apartment and told Ethan to take her home.

"Brooklyn what happened."

"That bitch is selfish and ungrateful, that's what happened."

Chapter Twelve

Some wounds have faces

Ethan walked Brooklyn to her door.

"Bay you've been quiet all night. Are you going to tell me what happened in there?"

Brooklyn tilted her head, "I like it when you call me bay."

Ethan placed his hands upon her face and kissed her. Chills traveled through Brooklyn's body as Ethan slid his hand down her back: he grabbed her ass smashing her against his hard body.

"Would you like to come in?" she asked.

Ethan nodded his head and took Brooklyn's hand in his.

****

Even though Lauryn couldn't come within a hundred feet of Thailand, he still had new locks on his home and business installed, along with cameras around the perimeters of his spa. Thailand thought that after what happened at Aaron's restaurant, his clientele would've declined, but it actually brought him more business. The spa was hectic. Thailand had given hour long treatments to five clients and it was only one in the afternoon.

"Michelle, I'm making my 1:30 appointment my last appointment. I need you to take my 2:45 all the way to my 5:00. And can you set up my space for me?"

"Sure thing Thai."

"Thanks Hun, you've always been my favorite."

"Mmm hmm."

Thailand went into his office and crashed on the couch. Aaron never told me how it went with him Derricka, he thought. He rustled through his phone for a while before he peeled himself off the couch to head to his appointment.

"Ugh. I don't want to!" he said bouncing up and down on his sofa.

Thailand walked into the room to find his client undressed and lying on the table. Just how I like it, he thought. He popped in a Nujabes cd and played his favorite track, 'The space between time'.

"Hello my name is Thailand, and I'll be taking care of you this afternoon. I understand that this is your first time here, so I will try to make it as pleasurable as possible."

Thailand began massaging her shoulders.

"What's your name ma'am?"

"Oh you don't have to call me ma'am. 50 years old is not that old."

"Wow your body looks great for 50, what's your secret?"

She laughed, "A lot of sex and plastic surgery."

"Sex and plastic surgery, huh? I can dig the sex part."

"You don't remember me do you Thailand?"

Thailand smiled, "No I don't recall us ever meeting."

She moved his hands and flipped onto her back.

"I told you that I would be back to get some of that dick when you got older, I just knew you would be blessed." Thailand stumbled back, knocking over a tray of oils.

"Ca ca Candice?"

"It's me in the flesh, now take those pants off." Thailand became so enraged that he grabbed Candice by her neck and lifted her off her feet. Candice started kicking and smacking Thailand, but he still managed to pen her against the wall.

"Bitch have you lost your mind? I should snap your fucking neck!"

Candice laughed aloud, "You forget that I like it rough Thai. Even as a child you were strong. Your endurance was amazing."

Thailand grabbed Candice by the hair and slammed her face against the door. She tried to kiss him, but he wrapped his hand around her face and walked her backwards out the front door.

"If you ever show your face around here again, I'll have you taken care of, do you understand?"

Candice laughed as she licked the blood from her bleeding nose.

"How are going to take care of me! When you couldn't even put that little thug in the ground like we asked you to fourteen years ago! YOU ARE WEAK! ALWAYS HAVE BEEN AND ALWAYS WILL BE!"

"GET THE FUCK AWAY FROM MY ESTABLISHMENT BEFORE I CALL THE POLICE!" Candice walked away laughing hysterically. When Thailand walked back into the spa, his entire staff was standing around shocked.

"GET BACK TO YOUR CLIENTS NOW!" he Thailand.

Hyperventilating, he collapsed on the sofa. Calm down Thai, calm down, he thought. After a couple of minutes, his breathing slowed. He had forgotten all about that night. When he was sixteen years old, his mom got into some deep debt with some drug dealers, so she offered Thailand to pay her dues. She convinced the men that Thai would do anything they asked him to without any fuss. It was dark and cold inside the building his mom took him to. Hypes were having sex in the hallway, while others were shooting up. Thailand and his mother walked down a few stairs into a basement where they were stopped by an oversized man.

"What are you here for?" asked the man.

"Shaky and Black are expecting us." his mother replied.

"Wait right here."

The man went inside the door and came back a few minutes later.

"Come in."

For the first time, Thailand saw how cocaine and crack was made. There were women in only panties and bras, with nets on their heads making the drugs. Thailand and Sahara walked to a table with four men, two of which had faces that would haunt Thailand for days to come.

"Sahara, I'm glad you made the right decision. I'm really happy that I didn't have to go looking for you." said Black.

"Never, I'm a woman of my word. This is my son. However you want him, however you need him he'll comply with no problems." Sahara assured them.

Shaky sat up in his chair.

"However we want and need him... Bitch do we look like we're gay?"

Sahara shook her head.

"We need him to murk this hustla named Ethan. He's fucking with our money, so we need him to disappear." said Shaky.

"We are gonna send some of our guys with him to rob Ethan, but we want your son to have the honor of killing him; If he gets it done, then your debt will be wiped clean. If not, we are gonna kill Ethan, you and your son. Got it?" Black asked.

"Yes I got it. When is this going down?"

"Tonight, so get him ready."

Sahara took Thailand's hand.

"Listen baby, you love your mama right?"

Thailand just stared at her.

"I need you to do this for me…I mean for us. You heard what those men said. They will haunt us down, find us, and put us in the ground."

Thailand snatched his hand away.

"Do I really have a choice Sahara?"

"Call me mama Thai. Just this once, just in case this is the last time."

Thailand ignored her plea and walked back over to the table.

"Can we get this over with?"

Black laughed, "I like this lil nigga he's ready to roll."

Shaky summoned four guys and told them where they could find Ethan. Thailand remembered the entire ride to 'L-Town'. They were drinking and smoking and he was trying his hardest not to puke. After a twenty minute ride, Thailand and the four men pulled up at the end of the Lotus and Bloomingdale block. They sat in the car and watched Ethan do work for a while before they gave Thailand the orders.

"Okay lil dude, that's Ethan in the fitted white sox hat. You're going to ask him for a bag of snow, and he's gonna tell you that it's a dub. You will hand him this ben, which will make him go in his pocket to get change. That's when we will beat his ass, take his money, and the rest of his work. Once we get him on the ground, you shoot him point blank in the dome with this nine." the driver instructed.

He handed Thailand the gun and told him to put it on his hip, then made him get out of the car.

"Remember what the bosses said. If Ethan lives, you and that crack head mama of yours are dead. Got it?"

The car reversed off the block, and Thailand walked towards Ethan. It felt like an eternity before he finally made it in front of Ethan.

"Yea dude what you need?"

Thailand stood there shaking.

"Aye man, tell me what you want or you have to move." said Ethan.

"I...I need a bag of snow." said Thailand.

"That's a dub homie."

When Thailand reached in his pocket, he accidentally revealed the nine. Ethan pulled out his piece and put it to Thailand's head.

"You trying to rob me nigga, who sent you?" Ethan asked.

"Shaky and Black said they'd kill me and my mother if I didn't kill you! They said that you're fucking up their money. My ma owes them money so your death would pay her dues." cried Thailand.

Next thing you know, Ethan was hit across the back with a steel bat. Ethan stumbled, but managed to keep his balance. Thailand closed his eyes and stood still, despite the sprinkles of blood he felt cover his face. He heard silence after the tenth gun shot. He opened his eyes to see all four guys lying in pools of blood. They were dead. Ethan was bleeding, but he grabbed his gun and started walking towards Thailand. Thailand broke out running and never looked back, literally. Earlier that day he went in one of his mother's latest lover's stash and took seven hundred dollars. He'd planned to leave Chicago, and this was his chance. He caught the blue line train to downtown and bought a greyhound ticket to Atlanta...

****

"Thailand, a woman named Adriana is here for you."

"Send her in please."

"Hello Thailand, Oh, were you sleeping?"

"No, come in, how you been?" he asked.

"I've been good. I just came by to see what was up with you. I heard you got sliced up at Aaron's."

"Yea, you women are psycho."

Adriana smiled, "Sometimes. So when can I make an appointment for a massage? I'm long overdue for one."

"I'm going on vacation, so it will have to be with one of the other therapists."

Adriana poked her lips out.

"Okay, okay how about tomorrow afternoon around three?"

"Yay! I'll be here. Don't have me waiting like you did at the restaurant." said Adriana.

"I'm so sorry about that. May I take you to dinner and make it up to you?"

"Well I'm hungry now, so let's go."

Thailand laughed, "I should have known you were straight forward after that poem you read at Aaron's."

"Yeah I was a tad bit frustrated with the male race at the time, but I'm over it. Well I'm over him." Adriana said.

"So what do you have a taste for? I want steak."

"Steak sounds good to me. Let's go. You think women are psycho now, we turn into exorcists when we're hungry."

Chapter Thirteen

After it all

     Thailand and Adriana ended up sitting by the Buckingham fountain, reminiscing on that night at Aaron's.

     "Ole girl is not going to jump from behind any of these bushes is she?" Adriana asked laughingly.

     "She can't come within one hundred feet of me, so we're good." Thailand continued, "So what was the angry poem about?"

Adrianna cleared her throat, "Well umm, I was dating this older man for three years. He bought me gifts, paid my bills, and to be 52 years old, he wasn't so bad in the bedroom. We would always argue about taking our relationship to the next level. He'd always say that he was married for many years, and it was a mistake, so he didn't want to make another mistake like that. He wanted to make sure what we had was right."

     "That sounds like a bunch of bullshit." said Thailand.

"That's because it was a bunch of bullshit. The man was still married."

"What!"

"Yep. He never divorced. I was just a side piece."

"What did you do when you found out?"

"I cursed him out, changed my numbers, residence, and cried." Adriana continued, "And he told me that he never had children, but come to find out, he has a son my age that he doesn't get along with."

"I can't really judge the man, because I've been quite the player myself. I've never been in a monogamous relationship before." said Thailand.

"Wow, well why not?" she asked.

"My childhood didn't really give me the option of being with one woman, but that's another story. Maybe if you stick around long enough, I'll tell you."

"Whether I stick around or not is up to you mister player." said Adriana.

"That's the thing, I don't want to live that life anymore. For the last few months I've been reflecting on my life, and all of my accomplishments. A wife and kids are the next and last things I care to achieve before I leave this world."

"I'm glad that you want to change. Love, love can be so beautiful. It can also cause you a lot of pain, but to me, it's all worth it in the end."

"Well I'll be thirty at the end of August, so it's time for me to be on my grown man shit."

"I really hope you are a man of your word, because I would love to get to know you better." said Adriana.

"I am a man of my word."

"What are you smiling for?"

"Your personality doesn't match your looks… And I like that." he answered.

"What is that supposed to mean?" she questioned.

"What I'm saying is that you seem very down to earth, despite the fact that your features are very exotic. Most women who are stunning like yourself, are extremely snotty and high maintenance. But I don't get that from you, and like I said, I like that."

"Good observation, because I'm not like that at all. This outfit I have on was thirty dollars and these heels were fifteen dollars. I'm not materialistic or superficial. I like to create my own style and my own things. I guess it's just the artist in me."

"Yeah I wanted to ask you when I'll get the chance to see some of your pieces."

"I'm having an art show in a couple of weeks at my studio. I'll email you all the info sometime this week. If you know any people who enjoy art, bring them along. If you don't, still bring people."

"Oh for sure, besides, Aaron loves art, especially pieces by this particular artist, so I know he will be down to come through." said Thailand.

"Cool, let's get going. It's getting cold by this water."

Thailand placed his jacket on Adriana shoulders, and suggested that they take the long way around so they could enjoy the moonlight before heading home.

Thailand looked up at the sky, "Man it's nice out tonight."

"Yes, yes it is." Adriana said gazing up at him.

****

Brooklyn was extremely nervous to watch Ethan fight tonight, and for the life of her she couldn't understand why. Ethan had one of his friends come pick her up to bring her to the venue. His friend showed her to her seat and told her that if she needed anything to text him. Brooklyn overheard a man saying that he bet against Ethan because his opponent was more polished and had more wins under his belt. Brooklyn was about to turn around in her seat to give him a piece of her mind, but the lights went dim.

The crowd went crazy when DJ Khaled 'All I do is win' started blasting. A group of men walked through the double doors surrounding a fighter who was jumping up down, and dancing to the music.

"Aye y'all know who it is! I might look pretty, but I'll drop these hammers on you. My name is muthafucking Jarod 'Steel Hands' James! And I'm about to smash dude's face in."

Jarod entered the ring and posed for pictures; in the middle of another one of his rants, the music changed from DJ Khaled to Lil Wayne's 'Right above it'.

Everyone went bananas as Ethan and his team walked in. Brooklyn couldn't see his face because he had on a black and white robe with the hood pulled down low. Brooklyn watched Ethan rotate his shoulders and wrists as he walked towards the ring. When he got to her seat, Ethan bent down and kissed her.

"Don't worry, I'm going to win."

Brooklyn nodded her head. As soon as Ethan stepped inside the ring, Jarod got at him.

"Look at this dude. Stepping in the ring all frowned up like Craig Mac's ugly ass. Who do you think you're spooking boy? I' ma soften that face up with these bricks I'ma lay on you. You hear me boy?"

Ethan stared at Jarod without responding. The announcer introduced the fighters and the referee. Ethan and Jarod met at the center of the ring.

"Okay boys, I want a clean fight. No head-butting, no hitting below the belt. Touch gloves. LET'S GO!" said the Referee.

Jarod jumped at Ethan to make him flinch, but was unsuccessful. He threw a right and Ethan ducked, giving him two left hooks in the ribs; Jarod buckled and hit Ethan in the groin when Ethan charged him.

"Illegal hit! Illegal hit! One more of those son, and a point will be deducted." warned the ref.

Ethan was ready to fight by the time Jarod came back to the center.

"Oh my bad homie, did that hurt?" teased Jarod. The Referee asked Ethan if he was okay, then told the men to fight. Someone in the audience called Ethan a bitch, so Ethan made the mistake of taking his eyes off of his opponent. Jarod threw a right hand straight down the pipe and stunned Ethan. Brooklyn gasped and covered her eyes. He got Ethan on the rope and worked his body. Joe was yelling at Ethan to get off the ropes. He must have heard Joe, because he used his forearm to push Jarod, and then he hit him with a hard overhand right. The crowed went crazy. Jarod could barely stand up straight. Ethan overwhelmed him with combinations to the body and head until the referee pulled him off of Jarod.

"That's enough son! That's enough!"

The man that bet on Jarod threw his hat on the ground and stormed out like a few others. Brooklyn couldn't believe how quickly Ethan turned into a beast like that.

"Omg, I think I'm turned on by this." she said.

The referee stood between the two fighters as the announcer revealed the winner.

"And the winner by knock out in the second round is Ethan Palmer!"

Brooklyn gave a standing ovation when the referee raised Ethan's hand. Ethan hugged everyone in his corner, then motioned for Brooklyn to come to him. She wrapped her hands around his neck and kissed him.

"I told you I would win." He said.

After pictures and an interview, Brooklyn waited for Ethan to meet her at the car. She saw a group of men approaching her who she thought was Ethan and his team, but it was Jarod and his.

"Damn you're sexy! What the fuck are you doing with that buster?" Jarod asked.

"Don't worry about who I'm with and what I'm doing with them." Brooklyn responded.

"Bitch don't get it twisted, your man won by luck. I'll beat his ass anytime, anywhere and then I'll fuck you for fun."

"You're not about to touch her homie." said Ethan. Jarod laughed, "Says who nigga?"

"Brooklyn get in the car."

"Ethan! You know the rules! No street fighting. He's not worth it. Let's go home." Joe said.

Ethan stepped in Jarod's face.

"If you ever come near my girl again, I'll split your fucking face right down the middle. Now you know I'm from the streets. Don't forget that. If I make one phone call I could arrange a fucking massacre. You know that don't you?" Ethan questioned.

Jarod smacked his lips, and he and his crew left. Ethan was furious when he got in the car.

"Joe, that muthafucka trying to make me return to the old me! Talking shit, threatening my girl, what the fuck?!"

"Ethan you've worked too hard to go back to that lifestyle. If you want him that bad we can ask for a rematch." said Joe.

Ethan turned to Brooklyn, "You okay?"

"Yes baby I'm fine."

Ethan pulled Brooklyn into his arms and they fell asleep on the way to her apartment.

"Kids wake up. We're at our destination." Joe said. Ethan walked Brooklyn to the door and kissed her goodnight. Walking into her apartment Brooklyn was pissed.

"Damn! I wanted some tonight! I'm wetter than a baby's bib! Shit!"

She was about to take off her shoes when her cell rang. It was Ethan.

"Baby let me in."

Brooklyn hung up and buzzed Ethan up to her apartment. As soon as she opened the door, he rained kisses upon her.

"Bay I want to make love." he said.

Brooklyn kissed him again and walked him to the bedroom.

Chapter Fourteen

Making love & Making up

"Turn your phone off, no interruptions." said Ethan. Ethan undressed and then watched Brooklyn do the same.

"Hurry up baby, take it off."

Brooklyn smiled at his impatience. His eyes narrowed as he grew frustrated. Ethan lifted her up and slammed her on the bed. He opened her legs and tore her panties off.

"Ethan! I just bought those!"

He destroyed her bra next. She gasped, turned on and frighten all at once. Ethan kissed her hard and aggressively.

"Give me." he whispered against her lips.

He left a trail of kisses from her lips to her inner thighs. Ethan used his fingers to spread her pussy lips and he began to move his tongue along her clit like a roller coaster.

"Oh my God, Ethan…" Brooklyn moaned.

He licked and sucked until she started to vibrate. Brooklyn pushed his head back and told him that it was his turn. She smiled at the size of Ethan. Damn he's about ten inches,

Brooklyn thought. She positioned herself on the side of him, and got to work. Jacking him off as she sucked the head of his dick. Every time she deep throated him, he moaned and yanked on her hair a little harder than before. When he couldn't take anymore, he grabbed her by the hair and bent her over. He whispered over and over, 'Give me' until he entered her. It was like they fit hand in glove. Ethan kissed her back before he started banging her with every ounce of strength he had.

"Shit, you are so tight and wet. This is my shit. You better not give my pussy away to anybody else."

Brooklyn was moaning uncontrollably.

"Baby I'm about to cum."

"Not yet, I'm not done." Ethan said.

He turned her on her back and penetrated her.

"Is it mine bay?"

Brooklyn kissed him, "Yes! Yes it's yours. I'm yours."

They made love until they both collapsed, falling asleep with him still inside of her.

****

Brooklyn had forgotten that she ran out of the house last night, leaving her computer on. She was awakened by someone sending her an instant message on Yahoo. Sometime during the night Ethan had rolled to the side of her, so it wasn't too difficult to wiggle from under him. Brooklyn moved the mouse to see that the message was from Derricka.

"Hey Boo, I called you last night, but your phone was off, so I hit you up on here. I miss my best friend. Call me okay? Bye… Love ya."

Brooklyn rolled her eyes and climbed back into bed with Ethan.

"Stop being stubborn and call her."

"WHAT THE FUCK?! How did you see that message all the way from over here, and I thought you were sleep." said Brooklyn.

Ethan laughed, "Baby I'm an ex thug. We don't sleep, we rest our eyes."

"Yea whatever, I don't have anything to say to her. Let's see how she feels when I return the favor of not returning her calls, or responding to her messages."

Ethan climbed on top of her and bit her chin. "Give me."
Brooklyn smiled and wrapped her legs around him.

****

The renovations on Aaron's were almost complete. In a few more weeks, the restaurant will be up and running like never before.

"So you're feeling Adriana huh? Aaron asked his friend.

"Yea she's a cool chick. We had a good time the other night. She invited me to an art show that she's having at her studio, which brought me to you." Thailand continued, "I know you're into art, so I figured I'd buy you a piece to put in your collection. You know, since I damn near burned your restaurant to ashes."

"Damn man, that's what's up. Yea I'd like to go. She's probably not as good as my favorite painter, but I'll give her a chance." Aaron said.

"Anyway, I told you about my time spent with Adriana, now it's your turn."

Aaron smiled. Thailand took a few steps back.

"Aaron…you hit that?"

"Man we almost broke the shower door."

"Aw shit! Aye let's go grab some beers because I want details!"

****

Derricka was leaving the mall when she tried Brooklyn's cell again. If this bitch don't answer her phone, I'm going make a pit stop at her house. She tossed all of her bags in the car and called Aaron.

"Hey honey what are you up to?"

They talked for a few minutes about their plans for the night, and about accompanying him to the art show.

"Of course I'll be your date to the art showcase. Who else would you take?"

After exchanging kisses, Derricka texted Brooklyn.

"Look BK, how long are you going to keep this up? You are being really unfair right now."

She was about to unlock the doors to her studio when a homeless woman approached her.

"Excuse me miss, could you spare some change?"

"Hold on, let me look in my purse..."

Derricka couldn't believe her eyes.

"Mama?"

The woman blinked numerous times before covering her mouth with a handkerchief.

"Derricka? Oh, oh my baby."

She went to hug Derricka, but she pushed her away.

"Derricka, baby, I know you must have a lot of questions. I'm so sorry. Leaving my girls was the biggest mistake of my life."

Derricka shook her head.

"Go beg someone else for change, because I don't have shit for your trifling ass."

Derricka walked into her studio completely ignoring the crying on the other side of the door: she went into her darkroom and broke down.

"How dare she think that I'd give her the time of day?! How dare she?!" Derricka said crying. She took out her cell and called Brooklyn. Brooklyn please pick up, I need you, thought Derricka.

"Hello?"

"Hello BK, can you meet me at my studio?"

"Derri what happened?!"

"Just meet me please."

Brooklyn hopped in her car scared to death from Derricka's call.

"I've never heard Derri cry before. I swear if Aaron has hurt her…" She said aloud. It usually took a half an hour to get to Derricka's studio from Brooklyn's apartment, but she made it there in fifteen minutes. She walked in frantically, calling Derricka.

"Derri! I'm here! What happened boo?!"

"BK I'm in here…the darkroom." Derricka replied. Brooklyn walked into the room to find Derricka sitting on the floor with a bottle of Jack Daniels.

"Derri are you okay?" asked Brooklyn.

"My father drank this all the time. He would drink a half a bottle before he would call me into his bedroom." Brooklyn continued to listen.

"He'd pour some on his penis and would have me suck it off and would do the same to me."

Brooklyn covered her mouth in disbelief. Derricka stood up and threw the bottle of Jack Daniels at the wall.

"He molested me! Made me play the role of his wife because that bitch left us!" yelled Derricka

"And then this bitch has the nerve to walk up and ask me for spare change! What about my innocence mama? Can we exchange my childhood for some change?!"

"Your mother is homeless?"

"Apparently so, I don't know how, and I don't know why, and I most definitely don't give a fuck."

Brooklyn hugged Derricka and began to cry.

"BK I'll be okay. I should've told you all of this before. And I'm sorry about what happened. I know you care about my well-being."

"Girl I'm crying because I haven't been completely honest with you either."

"Huh? What are you talking about?" Derricka asked.

"My childhood was rough as well. My mother is still with the man that abused me as a child. That's the real reason I don't talk to her. It's not because she's dead." Brooklyn admitted.

"Damn I guess we're both messed up." said Derricka.

Brooklyn wasn't in the mood to pour out her soul so she quickly changed the subject to one of the few things that she and Derricka loved... men.

"Okay enough of the sad stuff, what's going on with you and Aaron?"

Derricka laughed as she blew her nose.

"Girl we had sex that morning in the shower after our date, and we haven't stopped since!" Derricka continued, "Brooklyn he's great. The sex, the conversation, I mean, just all the time we've spent has been wonderful. It's not one dull moment when we're together, I love it! Oh you should come to Adriana's art show with us in a couple of weeks. Chile, Aaron loves him some art. He has pieces in every room of his house." said Derricka.

"That sounds fun. Ethan and I will be there." Derricka folded her arms.

"You and Ethan, the firefighter?"

Brooklyn nodded her head.

"BROOKLYN WHEN DID THIS HAPPEN?! OH MY GOD!"

"Girl let me tell you! I was at a bar with my co-worker Lana, when Ethan walked in. I walked over to him to thank him again for saving my life, and we've been hooking up ever since, but Derri, he put it on my ass last night! He's thick and long! And he knows how to work that tongue. He had a bitch vibrating all over the bed!"

The two laughed simultaneously.

"Hey. You know what will make us feel better? Brooklyn asked.

"Yep, let's go shopping!" Derricka replied.

"BK can we stop by Aaron's place? I want to give him these photos he's been hounding me for."

"What kind of photos Derri?" Brooklyn asked laughingly.

"Shut your freaky ass up! These are pictures of the city."

"Yeah, yeah, yeah, y'all better not try to get a quickie in when we get there." said Brooklyn.

When they got to Aaron's he was arguing with an older gentlemen.

"What the fuck did you come up here for Dad? To point out that my restaurant almost burned down?"

"You damn right! That's what your soft ass get, walking around here wearing aprons and cooking. What kind of shit is that?"

"Look old nigga, I stopped giving a damn about what you thought of me a long time ago, so your little attempts to degrade me is a waste of time. Now what you need to worry about is why my mother is so unhappy, since you were never a father, how about you be a husband to your devoted wife."

"Son you want to know why I was never much of a father to you?"

He leaned over and whispered in Aaron's ear.

"Because I never wanted you."

Enraged, Aaron punched his father in the face. Derricka and Brooklyn got out the car and ran over to Aaron.

"Aaron Baby what's wrong?! Derricka asked.

Aaron walked off.

"Aaron talk to me! What happened?"

"Nothing Derricka! Leave me alone!"

"Aaron baby I'm concerned. I'm just trying to be here for you."

"But did I ask you to be? I'm a grown ass man, I can take care of myself. Why are you here anyway?" asked Aaron.

"Muthafucka because she wanted to bring your goofy ass some pictures that YOU asked her for!" shouted Brooklyn.

Derricka stared at Aaron for a few seconds before she tossed the pictures at him.

"Don't ever in your life call my phone." she said.

"Do like my father did and get the fuck away from my business." he said.

Aaron watched Derricka and Brooklyn drive off.

"Damn! Why did I snap on her like that? My father brings out the worst in me! Shit!" he yelled.

Aaron called up Thailand to tell him what went down.

"Man Thai, I don't know why I let that man get to me. He made me so mad that I fucked around and cursed my baby out. Shit, I think we just broke up."

"Derricka seems like a good woman, so if she's worth it like I think she is, you'd bust your ass to get her back." said Thailand.

"Yeah you're right. I've waited a long time for a woman like her and I refuse to let another man cop that." Aaron said.

"I am supposed to meet up with Adriana for a movie, but if you need me to slide through..."

"No, no have fun, I'll talk to you later." said Aaron. Aaron hung up with Thailand and banged his head against the car steering wheel. If she wants this to work, she'll forgive me, thought Aaron. He took a deep breath and dialed Derricka's number.

Chapter Fifteen

It's about to go down

For the last two weeks, Derricka had been ignoring Aaron's calls, voicemails, and emails, but she was starting to miss him.

"Derri what are you thinking about?" asked Brooklyn.

"Aaron. I miss him so much."

"Then return his calls, with your cry baby ass." said Brooklyn.

"I thought you would want me to make him sweat…"

"Derri listen, any fool can see that you two are made for each other. You light up when you talk about him. I want you to be happy, and if forgiving him so you two can move on to bigger and better things will make you happy, then call him." said Brooklyn.

"Awe I love you girl."

"Okay okay, enough with the mushy stuff. Now let's get sexy for our men and show up those bitches that will be at the art show." Brooklyn said.

"Yea, they aren't ready for Derri and BK."

****

Ethan and Aaron pulled up to Brooklyn's apartment at the same time.

"What's up man? Aren't you the firefighter that saved Brooklyn?" asked Aaron.

"Yeah that was me. What are you doing here?" Ethan asked.

"I'm here for Derricka, not Brooklyn. So, you and BK are an item huh?"

"Yeah we are. Are you and Derricka?"

"Yeah that's my baby. Aye I didn't get your name."

"I'm Ethan."

"Nice to meet you Ethan, I'm glad it's on a happier note." Aaron said laughingly.

"Yeah me too man, what the hell is taking them so long?"

"Dog, these are women. Do you really have to ask?" The two men laughed and named other things that only women do.

"What's so funny fella?" asked Brooklyn.

"BK, don't start." said Aaron.

Brooklyn pushed past Aaron and wrapped her arms around Ethan's neck.

"Miss me bay?"

Ethan kissed her, "What do you think?" he answered. Derricka walked up to Aaron, "Hi."

Aaron embraced her.

"Damn how long are y'all going hug?! It's only been two weeks, shit!" said Brooklyn.

It took almost an hour to make it to uptown Chicago to Adriana's studio, and Brooklyn was pissed.

"I don't even know the bitch to be taking road trips to see her; what she got on the gas?!"

Brooklyn had everyone laughing all the way from the car until they entered the place.

"This shit better not be whack, that's all I have to say." Brooklyn said.

The couples split up to look around the gallery. Aaron glanced over a couple of pieces.

"Derri, these paintings look familiar. I mean from the brush strokes to the exaggerated facial features of the subjects." he said.

Aaron went to the bottom left hand corner of a painting and found the initials, A.J.

"Adriana is my favorite painter?"

"Damn it's a small world isn't it?" said Derricka.

"I want a couple of pieces in here. She's a wonderful artist. These paintings are beautiful." said Brooklyn.

"Whatever you want baby, you can have." said Ethan.

"Let's go find Derri and Aaron to see what they're getting." Brooklyn said, grabbing Ethan's hand.

When they walked to the other side of the studio, Adriana was standing in front of a large crowd.

"Thank you for coming through everybody. All of these paintings are exclusive pieces. Tonight is the only time and place that they've been displayed. Looking at these pieces is allowing you to look directly into me. Some of you might not like what you see. Some of you might be confused by what you see, while others will see themselves within my art. So let's discuss, let's drink, and write checks! Once again, I appreciate your attendance."

The audience clapped and began talking amongst themselves.

"Adriana, these people are raving about you. I have to admit, this is exciting." Thailand said.

"Yeah, I'm extremely happy at the turn out. Now go make me some money."

"I got you babe."

****

Ethan was drinking champagne when he noticed Thailand across the room.

"He looks very familiar to me."

"Who looks familiar?" asked Brooklyn.

"The dude over there in the cream button down." Brooklyn followed Ethan's eyes.

"Oh that's Thailand. He's Aaron's best friend. He caused the fire at the restaurant. Well not on purpose, but still..." Brooklyn said.

"No, I know him from somewhere else. I never forget a face."

"Well let's go over there and talk to him." Brooklyn suggested.

Grabbing her arm, Ethan yanked her back.

"No not yet. Let me think."

****

"Aaron baby, the three paintings you picked out comes to twenty thousand dollars. Should you spend that much money in one night?"

Aaron frowned, "Who asked you to be my logic? But yea you're right, I'll just get one for now."

"Thank you very much." said Derricka.

Ethan stood behind Thailand to hear his conversation. Thailand was expressing to another couple why the piece they were interested in purchasing was one of his favorites.

"I think this is a good choice. It can go in any room of the house, with the exception of the kitchen and don't worry, I'm not spitting game. I'm not into fucking up other people's money."

Ethan stopped in mid sip of his champagne. Those words echoed in his mind, 'fucking up other people's money'.

"Brooklyn, hold this glass."

Ethan tapped Thailand on the shoulder.

"What's up man, you thinking of finishing the job?" Ethan asked.

Thailand frowned, "Excuse me. Do I know you?"

"Yeah you know me homie. You tried to kill me when we were kids, remember?"

Thailand's glass shattered on the floor.

"E…Ethan?"

"Yeah it's me."

Brooklyn could see that Ethan was furious because he had the same look on his eyes in the boxing ring. She pushed her way through the crowd and found Aaron and Derricka.

"Aaron, Ethan is about to hurt Thailand! Apparently Thai tried to murder Ethan years ago." Brooklyn said frantically.

"What?! What the fuck?! Where are they?!" Brooklyn guided Aaron to where they were, then they saw a broken window, and Ethan on top of Thailand.

"Man I told you that night that I was forced to do it! Because if I didn't, they were going to kill me! I'm sorry man! I'm sorry!" Thailand said pleadingly.

"I should kill you! I should fucking kill you!"

"Ethan baby please, look at me. Can we talk about this?"

"Fuck that Brooklyn." Ethan yelled.

"What the fuck is going on?!" Adriana shouted.

Ethan kicked Thailand in the stomach.

"Answer her!"

"Fourteen years ago, I tried to kill Ethan. My mother was a drug addict and she was in debt with some big time drug dealers. In order for her debt to be wiped clean, I had to knock off their rival drug dealer, who was Ethan. If I didn't kill him, they were going to kill me and my mother, but I fled the state that night, so they didn't catch me." Thailand explained.

Everyone in the studio stood silently in shock.

"Now that's a man. You should've been in the army son. What's your name? Ethan? We could've used a cold mutha like you."

Aaron spun around, "Dad? What are you doing here, and who is that?"

Brooklyn couldn't believe her eyes, it was Lana.

"Lana what are you doing with Aaron's father? And he's married!" yelled Brooklyn.

"Anthony, you told me you were divorced and didn't have any children." said Lana.

"Yeah, that's the same thing he told me. That's why we are no longer together."

Everyone looked at Adriana.

Thailand stood up, "This is the older man you were in a relationship with for three years?"

"Three years?! Three muthafuck...You bastard! You've always treated my mother like shit!" screamed Aaron.

"Yes! And I will continue to do so. I pull the strings on your mother. Always have and always will."

Aaron lunged at Anthony, but was restrained by Ethan.

"Anthony, get your trifling ass up out of here! Get out of my got damn studio! Everybody get out! Get the fuck out!"

Brooklyn walked up to Anthony and smacked the shit out of him. Everybody stared at her.

"What?! What the he'll y'all looking at? Somebody needed to smack his stupid ass."

Chapter Sixteen

The Ugly Truth

Aaron was heated. He waited for Adriana to walk outside.

"So you're telling me that you were with my father for three years and not one thing pointed to him being married?" questioned Aaron.

"No Aaron I didn't know shi..."

Ethan cut in, "Adriana? Is that you?"

Adriana stared at Ethan.

"Ethan! Oh my God! Now I remember. You told me about that night, the night that Thailand was sent to kill you. How could I forget your face?"

She walked up to Ethan and hugged him.

"How do you two know each other?" asked Brooklyn.

"Ethan and I met on the streets when we were kids. I found him rummaging through a garbage can for food. I told him where to get a hot meal and we were friends ever since then." Adriana replied.

"Oh okay. Touching story, but enough with the touchy feely shit." said Brooklyn.

"Okay I need a drink." said Thailand.

"I think we all need a drink." said Brooklyn.

"Well I'm thinking of getting wasted, so might I suggest my house and everybody can leave in the morning?" Aaron said.

Everyone agreed except Thailand.

"I'll go only if Ethan doesn't try to kill me." Brooklyn looked at Ethan, practically begging him not to with her eyes.

"My girl just saved your life." said Ethan.

"Thank you Brooklyn."

Everybody loaded into their cars to head to Aaron's house. With Brooklyn driving, she and Ethan were going to beat Aaron back to the Westside.

"Damn baby, slow down." said Ethan.

Brooklyn smiled, "Don't ever tell me to slow down."

"You are so fucking nasty." Ethan said laughingly. Everyone trailed Aaron until Thailand's cell phone rang.

"Who's calling me from West Suburban Hospital?" Thailand answered his phone.

"Hello is this Thailand Moore?"

"Yes it is. May I ask what this call is in reference to?" Thailand replied.

"My name is Nurse Patrick, and I'm calling because your mother's last request was to talk to you. We don't think she's going to make it until the morning sir."

"Okay, I'll be there, Adriana go to West Suburban. I need to see my mother."

Thailand called Aaron, and everyone headed to the hospital. Thailand went to the front desk and told them who he was. The nurse told him what room and bed.

"Thai do you want me to go with you?" asked Aaron.

"No, I'll be alright. Be right back."

To Thailand, it felt like the longest walk he'd ever taken. When he got to the room, he stood in front of his mother's curtain before he opened it. When he pulled back the curtain he gasped at the condition of her body. She was so bruised from all of the drug usage over the years. She looked to be no more than ninety pounds, if that.

"Sahara? Sahara can you hear me? It's Thailand."

"She can hear you. She's just non responsive." Thailand turned to see a nurse.

"Hi, I'm Nurse Patrick. I'm the one who called." Thailand shook his head.

"She left you this letter and that box over there. I'll leave you two alone."

Thailand began reading the letter… a letter full of apologies and confessions. Thailand shot up in the chair; he couldn't believe what he had just read. "What the fuck? Aaron?" he said out loud. He leaned on her bed and broke down.

"You knew where I was all this time, but you wait until you're dying to come clean. You say that you love me, but the things you made me do to satisfy your sick craving for crack cocaine were outlandish and disgusting. You never threw me a birthday party or gave me a Christmas gift. I learned on my own, because you were too fucking high to take me to school. You used to get money for me

EVERY MONTH AND I DIDN'T SEE ONE DIME OF IT! And you want me to call you mama? For what Sahara?! For what?! When were you ever a mother to me?" He wiped his face and stood up, "I'm better than how you raised me. That means I have something that you never had…a heart. So I'm going to be the same ole good son like I've always been, and give you what you want."

Thailand was about to continue when the machines started going crazy. A doctor and a couple of nurses ran into the room, pushing Thailand out of the way. He watched them work on his mother until the doctor called it. At eleven thirty p.m., Sahara Alexandra Moore was pronounced dead. The doctors and nurses said something to him, but he couldn't hear them. He walked over to her lifeless body and wrapped his hands around hers.

"Goodbye mama." he said as he kissed her forehead. He grabbed the letter and box, and then found Nurse Patrick.

"Nurse she wants to be cremated…give her what she wants."

Thailand walked into the waiting room and everybody stood up.

"Are you okay?" asked Adriana.

"She's dead. I said goodbye, so I'm fine."

The women started crying, but it was Brooklyn who approached Thailand.

"Thai I'm so sorry." She hugged him, and kissed his cheek.

"Aaron, Anthony served for years in Thailand, and he used to talk about it to anyone, anywhere, right?"

"Yeah, he did."

"You told me once that you found coke in your dad's office when you were a child."

"Yeah I remember telling you that. Why? What's up?" questioned Aaron

"Well according to my mother, they met at a lounge, had an affair, and she was introduced to drugs through him. You weren't a year old when she got pregnant with me. She said he paid her to keep quiet."

"Thailand what are you saying?"

Thailand handed Aaron the letter.

"I'm saying that we're brothers."

Chapter Seventeen

Familiar Strangers

Everyone's mouths dropped.

"I can't believe we're all connected like this. This shit is crazy." said Ethan.

"Thai, you're telling me that we're brothers?" Thailand nodded. Aaron read the letter and grew angrier the further along he got.

"So much makes sense now. The times he wouldn't come home for days, the times where he would snap out of the blue, because he was high. The phone calls must have been from your mother. She'd call and hang up, or just breathe into the phone. Mom would never tell me why dad was dishonorably discharged, and now I know it had to be because of drugs."

Aaron sat down and looked at Thailand.

"It always bugged me why I felt so close to you. I mean no homo, but I've always thought of you like a brother." Aaron admitted.

"Y'all I really need that drink." said Thailand."
When they arrived at Aaron's house, they broke out bottles
of liquor before they even kicked off their shoes.

"Aaron, what do you have to eat up in this joint? I'm
starving." Brooklyn asked.

"It's some of everything in there. You could make a
five course meal if you wanted."

Brooklyn looked around.

"Ladies y'all want to whip up something to eat?"
They all agreed and went to work on a late night dinner.

"Damn Thai, we're brothers." said Aaron.

Thai threw back a shot of Ciroc.

"Yep, and to be honest, I'm not tripping, because
you've always been my partner in crime; that is not going to
change." Thailand said.

"How did you two meet?" asked Ethan.

"I decided to ditch school one day in seventh grade,
due to peer pressure by some classmates. They were
drinking and smoking blunts, so I wanted to try. One of the
kids I was with said that he knew of a weed head named
Chummy that would buy herb for him all the time, as long

as he paid for it and let him hit the blunts. All of us that ditched headed to the liquor store on Central and North Ave to meet up with Chummy, when I saw Thai out there macking four chicks at once."

"Aye! It was five! The fifth one hopped on the bus before you came." said Thailand.

Rolling his eyes, Aaron continued.

"Anyway, I was never good with the ladies, so it fascinated me how he got all of their numbers AND they'd go inside the liquor store to buy him shit. He kissed ALL OF THEM before they walked off. It was crazy, so I approached him and asked how in the hell did he do that?" He looked at Thai, "And you said…"

"I said that I was born to be a player. It's natural for me. I mean look at this handsome face and sexy smile." They all laughed.

"Psh! Please! Playa my ass!" said Brooklyn, "Let's go! Dinner's ready."

Thailand and Aaron looked at Ethan.

"Good luck with that man." Thailand said.

The fellas walked into the dining room to find steak, rice, vegetables, bread, and wine awaiting them.

"Damn! How do we have grilled steak with no grill?" questioned Aaron.

"Aaron you have a griddle. That's how we made the steaks. Now everybody hold hands and let's bless this food." Brooklyn demanded.

"Uh I would like to lead the prayer, if y'all don't mind." said Thailand.

Everyone bowed their heads.

"Dear Heavenly Father, we would like to thank you for bringing us together for this glorious meal. It is because of you that we are all in good health and good spirits, and we would like you to continue to bless us as you always have, in Jesus name, amen."

They talked and laughed as they all got to know each other better. Three bottles of Moscato later, it was six in the morning.

"Damn y'all we need to get some sleep. Thailand and Adriana is on the floor knocked out." said Derricka.

"Ethan and Brooklyn, y'all can take the bedroom up the stairs to the right, and I'll wake these two drunks up and send them to the bedroom down here." Aaron said.

Brooklyn laughed, "If I wasn't exhausted, I'd record him snoring with his mouth open, and her drooling."

Ethan frowned, "Is that why Thailand's arm is wet? I thought she was sweating."

They laughed simultaneously.

"See you guys when we wake up." said Derricka.

"Okay boo, later." said Brooklyn.

Ethan and Brooklyn headed upstairs while Aaron tried to wake Adriana and Thailand up.

"Baby they are out for the count. Just toss a blanket on them and let's go to bed." said Derricka.

Aaron did as she suggested, and just for laughs she snapped a picture.

"This is for Brooklyn." Aaron said laughingly.

Chapter Eighteen

Apologetic

It was around 2 P.M. when Thailand awakened next to Adriana.

"Lord please tell me its sweat that I feel on my arm."

He managed to slip his arm from under her and wiped it on her pants. Thailand was on his way to the kitchen to get a glass of water when he accidentally kicked the box. "Ouch! WHAT THE FUCK?!" He picked up the box and sat down on the couch. What is in here Sahara? He thought. When he opened it, the first thing he saw was an envelope with 'Thailand and Mommy' written on it. He opened the envelope to find his birth certificate and pictures of her bathing him in the kitchen sink while making funny faces with him. All he could think was how happy and beautiful she looked. He placed the pictures back in that envelope and grabbed the second one that read, 'Thailand's achievements'. In this envelope, there were certificates and paper awards he had accumulated in grammar school. Wow, I didn't know she kept all this stuff. I thought for sure she'd thrown it away, he thought. With a smile on his face, he picked up the last envelope. It said 'Thailand's family'. There were pictures of men and women with long dreadlocks. Some in the midst of prayer, and others smoking cannabis. There was this one photo of a young couple holding a baby. At the bottom it said, 'Amoy, Nadir, and baby Sahara'.

"Wow, I look just like my grandfather." said Thailand. There was much more on the Rastafarian movement and the history of Jamaica. Thailand went into his jacket pocket and pulled out the letter Sahara wrote. In it was the phone number and address to his grandparents. "I have to contact them."

"Contact who?" asked Adriana.

"Oh, I thought you were asleep, my grandparents. I need to go see them. I never met them before."

"I think they'll be happy to meet you for the first time." said Adriana.

"Yeah I hope so. I'm hungry. Let's go raid the fridge." Thailand said.

They walked into the kitchen to find Aaron feeding Derricka.

"You two disgust me. What's for breakfast?" Thailand said.

"Shit. I need all y'all to bounce so I can enjoy my baby." said Aaron.

"Now that's just nasty." said Brooklyn.

Ethan laughed, "Aaron we're leaving anyway. Brooklyn has papers to grade, and I have to go train for my upcoming fight."

"Hey Aaron when will your restaurant reopen?" asked Adriana.

"Oh yea! I meant to tell everybody. Next Friday Aaron's will be back open for business!"

"I know everybody will be there, right?" Derricka said.

"Of course we will. We have to support the family." Thailand assured her.

"And we are going to have our first erotic poetry night that Friday. It's all about the grown, sexy, and freaky!" said Aaron.

"We'll most definitely be there Aaron, but right now we have to go so give me hugs." Brooklyn said.

"I'll walk you guys out." Derricka said.

Just as Derricka opened the door, Anthony was about to knock.

"Hello, is my son here?"

"And which son would that be player, Aaron or Thailand?" Brooklyn asked.

Ethan put his hand over her mouth.

"Well I guess both of them." said Anthony.

"Dad what are you doing here?" questioned Aaron.

"Well I came to talk to you son. Can I come in?"

Aaron nodded, and directed Anthony into the living room.

"What is this about?"

"Aaron it's about everything, me, you, Thailand…everything." Anthony was about to continue, but Thailand walked in.

"Hello son. Have a seat. You need to hear this as well."

"I'll stand Anthony." said Thailand.

"Okay, look. After hearing of Sahara's passing, I came to my senses and came clean to your mother, Aaron. She cried and told me that she knew already. She was just waiting for me to be a man and admit my infidelities. Aaron she left me. I came home today and she was gone. Well I know you're thinking, why I even care when I've done nothing but cheat on your mother. I care because believe it or not, I love your mom. Always have and always will. She has been by my side through everything, including my drug addiction. That's where your mother came in Thailand. I want to apologize to you personally, from father to son, for turning your beautiful mother into a crack fiend. She was a student working as a librarian when I met her. Intelligent and sweet as pie, but I was a man that wanted to conquer her like everything else in my life, so I controlled and ruined her…in the end, damaging you. I was a young fool. I actually wanted you Thailand, but I couldn't risk my marriage. I paid Sahara to keep quiet about you. I wasn't a good father to Aaron, hell Thailand…I wasn't a father to you at all. Thailand all the things you had to go through being two drug addicts' son was fucked up and I'm so sorry. Aaron I'm sorry for the beatings and verbal abuse. I really do love you son. I love both of you...."

Anthony was weeping so uncontrollably that he couldn't speak any further.

"Because I am at peace with myself and childhood, I'll forgive you Anthony, but I will not call you dad, just like I never called Sahara mom. I'm an orphan and always will be." Thailand turned and walked out of the door.

Aaron stood in front of Anthony, and pointed towards the door.

"Well I'm not at peace with shit. So the forgiveness you seek will not be found here." Aaron stated.

Anthony wiped his face and stood at the door.

"Aaron I am sorry. I love you son."

A few minutes of silence passed before Aaron said goodbye to everyone.

"Aaron, Baby…are you okay?" asked Derricka.

"No. Let's get in bed and order some movies and food."

"Whatever you want honey, whatever you want."

Later that night, Aaron received a call from his mother saying that when she came home to get the rest of her things, she found Anthony dead in his study. He had shot himself directly in the heart.

Chapter Nineteen

Some things never change

That following Friday was bittersweet. Sweet because the doors to Aaron's restaurant were scheduled to open that night, and bitter because he had to bury his father earlier that day. It was a sunny, but a sad day as Aaron held his mother's hand while they lowered his father into the ground. Aaron watched his mother the entire morning, waiting for a tear to fall, or an outburst, but it never happened. Everyone met up at Aaron's home for the repast. Relatives he hadn't seen in ages were asking him for money, and to throw free parties at his restaurant. Aaron snapped and escaped to the patio.

"Are you alright Aaron?"

"Yea mom, I'm fine."

"Son, when did you start lying to me?"

Aaron dropped his head.

"Look baby, your daddy was an asshole. He burnt a lot of bridges and hurt a lot of people. Nobody here but you and me who truly care that he's gone."

Aaron turned around and embraced his mother.

"Mama, why didn't you cry? Not one tear."

"Because that fool left me all cried out."

It was 5 P.M. when everyone finally left Aaron's house. Aaron laid across his bed and stared at the ceiling.

"You aight big bro."

"Damn that sounds weird. I thought everyone left." Aaron said laughingly.

"Yeah they did, but I wanted to make sure you were cool. Another thing that's weird is that I'm literally an orphan now. Both of my parents have passed on." said Thailand.

"I'm real sorry about that Thai."

"It's all good. As long as you and my grandparents don't die no time soon, because y'all all I got."

Aaron gave Thailand a hug.

"Okay enough of that! Get dressed and I'll meet you at the restaurant." said Thailand.

Aaron let Thailand out and called Derricka.

"Hey Derri why did you leave?"

"Oh I'm sorry baby, but Ethan and I are looking for Brooklyn. She darted out of the repast like a bat out of hell. She just jumped in her car and sped off. She's not answering her phone and Ethan is livid!"

"What?! Where was I when this happened?!"

"It was right after you stormed out. Look babe, we'll meet you at the restaurant."

"Okay keep me posted."

Aaron stood in front of his closet and shook his head.

"If it's not one thing, it's another."

****

Brooklyn was speeding down the expressway trying to make it to her mother's house in Markham, Il. She had received a call from her mother saying that her boyfriend was trying to attack her baby brother, and if she could come and pick him up. She finally arrived to find the front door open, and furniture tossed.

"What in the world?!" Brooklyn asked incredulously.

Her mother had just dodged a flying cordless phone.

"I'm sick of this nigga! Always downing me! Telling me I ain't nothing and that I never will be!" screamed Brooklyn's brother, Marcus.

"That's because you a lazy bum! You don't do shit but sit on your ass all day!"

"Don't say that to him! That's your son." said Brooklyn's mother.

"Marcus get your things and let's go."

"Who the fuck called her over here like she's going to beat my ass or something?"

Her mother's boyfriend stepped to Brooklyn and asked her the same question directly.

"Look dude you already know what it is. I ain't never been scared of you, and I'm not about to start now. So I suggest you back up out my face." warned Brooklyn.

"Or what, because I will beat your ass like I used to…remember?"

And Brooklyn did remember. All the days and nights he choked her, bruised her by throwing her into walls and across rooms. Abusing her right in her mother's face, the hell he made her childhood to be. He was the monster that never disappeared. Acting on pure emotion, Brooklyn punched him in the face, and they began fighting. He grabbed Brooklyn by the throat and slammed her into the wall. Her mother screamed. Marcus was trying to get his father off of her, but Brooklyn had to swing her way out as usual. It seemed like forever before they were separated.

"Get this bitch out of my house!"

"Brooklyn! I called you over here to get your brother, not to start shit!" yelled her mother.

"What the fuck?! This nigga stepped to me! Why don't you ever make him responsible?! It's always Brooklyn's fault. You let him do whatever he wanted to me, because your weak ass don't want to be alone. You're selfish as hell! Always choosing dick over your seeds. Well I hope that piece of dick that you defend so hard takes care of you when you can't even wipe your ass anymore, because I'll fuck around and leave your ass to rot!" Brooklyn continued, "When my grandmother died, my mama died. You are Lisa from now on, because you never earned the title 'mom'. Don't ever in your fucking life call my phone again. I don't deal with raggedy ass people like y'all!"

Brooklyn grabbed her purse and stormed out, forgetting her reason for going over there in the first place.

"Damn, when Ethan sees my face, he is gonna flip." Brooklyn said while looking in the mirror. She sped off and decided that she was going to enjoy Aaron's erotic poetry night, and forget that this ever happened.

Chapter Twenty

Where is the love?

When Brooklyn pulled up to her apartment, Ethan was sitting outside.

"Brooklyn where have you been? Why didn't you answer the phone?"

Brooklyn hugged Ethan and broke down. He lifted her face and kissed her.

"Bay, tell me what's wrong." Ethan begged.

Brooklyn opened the door and stood on the hallway under the light. Ethan hit the fan.

"Who the fuck…what the fuck…who did this?!" Brooklyn told Ethan everything from the beginning. The more she told, the more he got upset. By this time, they were inside her apartment arguing.

"Ethan I don't need you yelling at me right now! You are supposed to be comforting me, not criticizing me!"

"Why would I comfort you when you did something stupid?! What would possess you to go over there alone, when you know how he is? What were you trying to prove Brooklyn?!"

"I wasn't trying to prove shit! I went to remove my little brother from a situation that NO ONE EVER CARED TO REMOVE ME FROM!"

"That is no excuse! You are a woman. You have no business fighting a man..."

"AND HE'S A MAN THAT HAS NO BUSINESS FIGHTING CHILDREN AND WOMEN! I'm so sick of everybody not holding him responsible! You and my mother are making this my fault and it's not!"

Brooklyn was crying, but Ethan showed no concern.

"Ethan you act like you don't care." cried Brooklyn.

"Why should I when you endangered yourself on purpose?"

Brooklyn was stunned by what she had just heard.

"FUCK YOU ETHAN! FUCK EVERYBODY! ALL YOU MUTHAFUCKAS ARE RAGGEDY!"

"I can see why he used to beat your ass, and why he beat it tonight, BECAUSE YOUR MOUTH IS OUT OF CONTROL!"

Brooklyn just stood there. It felt like she was going to faint. She walked past Ethan, grabbed her keys, and left. She hopped in her car and drove for hours. She finally chose a destination and rang her grandfather's doorbell.

"Hey my little baby, it's late. You okay?"

Brooklyn started crying and her grandfather walked her in. Brooklyn couldn't talk or eat, because she was exhausted. She went to bed hungry, emotionally drained, and in physical pain. She knew she wasn't leaving this bed anytime soon.

****

Ethan walked into Aaron's upset with himself. He couldn't believe how mean he was to Brooklyn; he felt helpless and less than a man, all because the woman he love was beat up. Derricka saw Ethan when he walked in, and met him at the door.

"Hey E, heard anything?"

"Yeah, she came home. We argued about her going to her mom's house and fighting her boyfriend. I said some mean things, and she ran off again. I really fucked up Derri."

"Well what did you say?" asked Derricka.

Ethan told her exactly what he said, and Derricka stumbled back.

"Oh My God Ethan! No! No you didn't say that! How could you?!"

Derricka had tears in her eyes. She told Ethan how unbelievable he was, and walked off.

"Aaron baby, it's worse than I thought. Brooklyn's hurt. Her mom's boyfriend beat her up, and Ethan made it worse."

"Okay okay, calm down. We'll look for her okay? I'll have Thailand make sure everything runs smoothly, and then he can meet us."

Aaron broke everything down to Thai, and he and Derricka left.

"Derri, is she still not answering?"

"No and I've already called some mutual friends of ours, but they haven't talked to her. I can't think of anyone else right now."

After hours of calling, Derricka and Aaron called it a night.

"Don't worry babe, she'll call back tomorrow." Aaron assured her.

****

Brooklyn slept an entire day before her grandfather woke her up.

"BK, wake up baby. You have to eat something. Come on open your eyes and look at me."

He had a bowl of homemade chicken noodle soup, which was her favorite.

"Open up Brooklyn."

He fed her about five spoons of soup before she laid back down to sleep.

"I'll be back in the morning to check on you."

He kissed her on the forehead, and left the soup on the nightstand in case she got hungry.

It had been a day and a half since anyone had heard from Brooklyn, and Derricka was sick to her stomach.

"Ethan, I wonder if she's..."

"No she's not Derricka. Don't even think that. Now think. I know she has to have an aunt, uncle, cousin, somebody that knows where she is." said Ethan.

"Her grandfather! Ethan she always told me that whenever she was hurt, she would go to her grandparents' for comfort. He lives in the south suburbs, in Country Club Hills. We can try him."

"Well let's go."

They picked up Aaron and headed to the suburbs. For the entire ride Derricka was reassuring Ethan that Brooklyn would forgive him, because she loved him.

"Derricka how do you know that she loves me?" questioned Ethan.

"Because she's never been so into a guy in her life! She talks about you all day. She thinks about you all day. She can't see you two not being together. She feels the same way I feel about big head back there."

Aaron laughed, "Which head you talking about baby?"

"What's so crazy is that I love her too. I've never felt this way before. I don't know why I would ruin it like this."

"Ethan look, we're almost there. Once she sees you, everything will be fine." said Derricka.

"Wait! I can't go over there empty handed. We just passed a flower shop. I'm going to turn around."

Ethan purchased a huge card and a dozen sunflowers, Brooklyn's favorite. When they pulled up to Brooklyn's grandfather's house, they didn't get out immediately.

"Okay y'all, no fussing with her. Let's show her some understanding and love. You hear me Ethan?" Derricka asked.

"You act like she's in there!"

"Ethan shut…up! And knock on the door."

Ethan knocked a few times before someone opened the door.

"Hello, may I help you?"

"Hi, we're looking for Brooklyn, she's gone missing."

"Well who are you people?"

"I'm her boyfriend Ethan, and this is her best friend Derricka and her boyfriend Aaron."

Brooklyn's grandfather walked away from the door and motioned for them to come in.

"She's back here sleeping. She hasn't left the bed since she got here."

They all entered a dark room where the only light shining was from the hallway. Derricka sat on the bed and brushed Brooklyn's hair. Brooklyn opened her eyes and stared at Derricka.

"Hey boo, how you feeling?"

"How did you find me?" Brooklyn asked.

"I did some hard thinking, and thought of your safe place, which is with your grandfather."

"Brooklyn, baby we came to take you home."

"Ethan, I'm not going anywhere with you. We are done. We're over."

"Baby no we're not."

"YES WE ARE!"

"NO WE'RE NOT! NOW LISTEN!"

Ethan kneeled on the side of the bed and grabbed Brooklyn's hand.

"Bay I'm so sorry. The things I said were out of line and I promise you, I won't ever hurt you like that again. I love you and I'm not leaving without you."

"You think you can just come here and use those sweet words, stare at me with those beautiful eyes, and expect me to say okay Ethan I forgive you for saying I'm to blame for my abusive childhood? Do you think bringing me a card and my favorite flowers will take away the fact that you credit these bruises on my body to stupidity? Well you have me mistaken Ethan. I love you, but not so damn much that I'll be with someone that made me feel worthless. Now get your ass out of my granddaddy's house."

"I'll be in the car." said Ethan as he walked out.

"BK, we're worried about you, so will you please come with us?" Aaron asked.

"When I'm ready, I'll contact you all, but until then… I'm on hiatus." said Brooklyn.

Derricka started crying.

"BK I love you. Call me soon."

"I love you too. Now close the door on your way out."

Chapter Twenty One

Can't live without you

Ethan had barely eaten or slept since seeing Brooklyn last. It was going on three weeks and he felt like he was the biggest screw up in the world, and he didn't want be without her. He couldn't be without her.

"Ethan! Focus! He was about to take your head off. Where is your head?!" screamed Joe.

"Nowhere Joe, I'm here."

"Boy I've been training you for a long time, so I know you. What's going on?"

Ethan explained what happened, and how the entire situation had him messed up.

"Son, if you love her like you say, then don't give up on getting her back. I went through hell to get my wife back. Well we were just dating, but when she left me, I knew that I wanted her to be my wife. 20 years later, she's still my wife." Joe continued, "Look, just clear your head for the fight and, and after that we'll devise a plan to get your wife back."

Ethan chuckled, "A plan and my wife huh?"

"Yep now get back in the ring and beat your sparring partner up like usual." Said Joe.

****

"Brooklyn, Aaron said he talked to Ethan, and he's hurting bad. He loves and needs you girl. People mess up all of the time, but are you so willing to throw away something you've been praying for over a mistake?" asked Derricka.

"Damn whose side are you on Derri? The things he said cannot be taken back."

"Okay I'm about to be real with you, and hit you with some tough love. Brooklyn you are always looking for a reason to hold a grudge. Everybody is not out to hurt you. Everybody is not your mom and her boyfriend. I don't know why you always find a reason to cut people off, but you need to stop because one day people are going to say they don't give a fuck if you are in their lives or not. You need to get your ass up, and let's go watch Ethan fight tonight. Come back to your place, rock his world, and live happily ever after. You love him, so you need to face it and tell him."

"I hate it when you're right. I guess I push people away so they won't hurt me, and I do need to tell him how I feel."

"Thank you! Now let's get sexy and go cheer your man to victory."

Ethan asked Joe if he had seen Brooklyn in the audience, but to his dismay, she wasn't.

"Ethan focus! You can't think about her right now. Listen I'ma say this, if she loves you, she'll come PERIOD! Now lets go." said Joe.

After warming up, it was soon time for the fighters to enter the ring. When it was Ethan's turn to walk to the ring, he looked at the seat he reserved for Brooklyn, but she wasn't there. Damn, he thought. He knew he had to focus and quick, because his opponent was a tough one who's been on a 10-0 winning streak. Ethan took a deep breath and stepped to the middle of the ring.

****

"Damn Derri we're going to be late. He's probably looking for me." said Brooklyn.

"BK he'll be fine. When he sees you in the crowd he's going win for sure for his baby."

****

Joe was yelling at the top of his lungs.

"Ethan put your hands up and stay off the ropes!" Ethan was getting pummeled. His opponent was relentless…Hooks and uppercuts were on point. Luckily for Ethan, he has a good chin. The bell finally rang to end the second round. Joe splashed water on Ethan's face.

"Ethan what is wrong with you?! Do you not realize that you are in a fight? Dude is whipping your ass! Here, drink some water."

Joe smacked him, "Pull yourself together before they take your ass out of here on a stretcher."

****

"Derri you know how nervous I am watching him fight. I hope he's winning."

"He is! Now come on before we miss another round."

Brooklyn and Derricka walked in and the place was full of 'Oooo's and Ahhh's from the action going on in the ring.

Ethan hit his opponent with a combination, but it didn't faze him. He made the mistake of dropping his hands, leaving his face unprotected.

"Oh no! Ethan's hurt!" The Commentator shouted.

"ETHAN! ETHAN GET UP!" Brooklyn was screaming.

The Ref began his count. Ethan looked dazed, struggling to get to his feet. The crowd was going wild. Through blurred vision Ethan saw Joe pointing at Brooklyn. Ethan stood straight, and shook his head yes when the Ref asked if he was good to fight. When the bell rang, Brooklyn ran to the ring.

"Ethan baby are you hurt?"

"Ethan can you still fight? If not, I can throw in the towel." said Joe.

"No! I can fight Joe. I want to fight."

"That's my boy! A warrior for life! Now go put his ass to sleep."

"No problem. I'm going to win baby, watch." Brooklyn smiled and went back to her seat.

"Ethan better get to work because he's down two rounds. Lavell Howard is no punk. He's here to win." said the commentator.

Both fighters jogged to the center of the ring at the sound of the bell. It seemed as if Ethan had gotten a second wind, because his movements were sharper and his punches were harder. Ethan won the next two rounds by out-boxing Howard. It was the beginning of the fifth round, and Ethan hit him with a teeth chattering uppercut and a devastating over hand right, knocking his opponent to the canvas.

"Oh My God! I don't know if Howard will get up! He's hurt!" said the commentator.

Lavell stumbled to his feet, but fell back down. The referee waived his hands to end the fight. Ethan jumped on the ropes waving his hands in victory.

"And the winner by knockout...Ethan Palmer!" Ethan hugged his corner and motioned for Brooklyn to come inside the ring.

"See baby I told you I'd win, piece of cake." Brooklyn laughed and gave him a long kiss.

"I love you Ethan."

"I love you too bay...a lot."

Ethan had Brooklyn and Derricka pose in a few pictures with him before they left the venue. After all the congratulations and an interview, they finally got the chance to go home.

"Baby can you drive? I'm kind of sore." Ethan asked.

"Yeah, no problem. When we get to my place, I'll feed you...then rub you down."

"Ewww too much information." said Derricka.

"Hating ass." Brooklyn and Ethan said in unison.

"That was a close fight son. I'm so used to you demolishing your competition. It was very interesting to watch you work for a win."

Everybody turned around to see a female version of Ethan.

"Long time, no see Elise, I can't say that I'm ecstatic to see you."

"Awww now Ethan, Elise? How about mama?"

"Well you would have to be one to get called one, wouldn't you?"

"Well son a lot changed when you left.."

"No, when you kicked me out for, according to you, looking too much like my father."

"Okay son, you're a grown man now. It's time to move on from that."

Brooklyn and Derricka both said 'What the fuck?" at the same time.

"Move on? Oh I moved on the day that it happened. I'm too strong for pettiness. If I was a weak dude, I wouldn't have been able to survive having no parents and the streets."

"Excuse me bay, but I have to ask, why did you hate his father so much that you would put your son on the street?" Brooklyn questioned.

"Unfortunately I did. I was in love with that man. I thought everything was perfect until he left me when you were a year old. I tried to ignore the fact that he had his father's nose, mouth, and ears, but I couldn't after so long. I made a bad parenting decision and abandoned my only child. I drove past the gym on Lake Street one day and I saw you training with Joe. I've been watching you fight ever since."

"Yeah Elise, this is all so very touching, but umm, I don't give a fuck. If you don't mind, I'm tired and ready to go home. I'm not in the mood to bask in your presence."

Ethan grabbed the ladies and led them to the car.

"Ethan, Joe told you he was married! Have you ever seen a ring? Have you ever seen his wife? Did you ever wonder why out of all his fighters, you're the only one that he calls son?"

Ethan turned around and walked back to Elise.

"I have pictures of you as a baby with him teaching you how to make a fist and put up your dukes."

Elise dug into her pocket.

"See look Ethan."

Ethan took the pictures out of her hand. He couldn't believe it. He was with his father all this time.

"I approached him one day and told him I would take him for child support, and tell you who he was if he didn't take care of you; yes Ethan I hated you both and I'm sorry."

"But why tell me all this now?" asked Ethan.

"Because it has been a long time coming, so I decided to let you know."

Ethan walked past Elise and went back into the venue. When he saw Joe, he punched him right in the face.

"All of this time you knew! You knew you were my father and you never said shit!"

"Because Elise didn't want me to, she knew I was on the come up with my boxing career, so she threatened to ruin it if I said anything."

"Well things can stay the way they've been. You're just Joe to me, and she's just Elise."

"Son, I'm sorry, I'm so sorry. If I can take every single thing back, I would. I wouldn't have left your mother in the first place. It was so much pressure not to settle down, so I got caught up in that life. I made sure the passion for boxing was strong between us. You fight so much better than I did."

"Is that why you cry after all my victories?"

Joe stood up from the floor.

"Yeah son, because you make me proud, always have. I mean shit, you were a mean ass hustler, but in that, I was better. Son, I'm asking you to forgive us."

"Let me sleep on it. I'll see you later Pops."

"I like that…'Pops'. I'll see you later son."

Ethan ran back outside.

"Leave your info with pops, and I'll let you know if I want a relationship with you."

"Sounds like you've forgiven him and not me, which was to be expected."

"I won't say I forgive him, but at least he apologized for abandoning me. You just told me to get over it. So I hope you get over it, if I never call you."

"I hope you do son. I hope you do."

"Maybe…maybe not mom…we'll see."

"You called me mom." Ethan walked away leaving his mother standing in the parking lot.

"Ethan, you don't look angry anymore." said Derricka.

"That's because I'm not. I finally got closure, and I'm relieved. I partially moved on, but now, I can truly put this behind me."

Brooklyn smiled at Ethan's newfound peace, while Derricka was thinking how she needed to confront her parents and forgive so she could have closure herself.

Chapter Twenty Two

I forgive you

Derricka sat in her studio and thought about how blessed she was. She had a successful career as a fashion photographer, a wonderful man who's also a successful business owner, and great friends. Friends both old and new, but somehow a slight feeling of emptiness crept inside of her. Derricka grabbed her keys, locked up her studio, and jumped in her car. It's probably a long shot, but I'm going to see if she's out here, Derricka thought. She drove around for 45 minutes before she decided to give up. As she was sitting at the light, she saw some kids kick over a homeless person's cart before running off. The person spun around and yelled, "Come on! Lord!" Derricka could see it was her mother. She found a parking space two blocks down, and got up the nerve to approach her.

"How did you end up this way?"

"Chasing after dreams that I didn't deserve."

"Were those dreams more important than raising your daughters, mama?"

"Unfortunately at the time, I thought they were." Blinking back tears, she finally turned to face Derricka.

"Derricka I'm so sorry, but your father was so controlling and verbally abusive that all I could think about was getting away. I realized a long time ago that making that decision was selfish, and the biggest mistake I've ever made in my life."

"What do you want…a hug?" asked Derricka.

"No…just forgiveness baby. All I want is for you and the rest of my babies to forgive me."

"You want to be forgiven? Well why would I do that?"

"Because I'm your mother."

"AND THAT DIDN'T MEAN SHIT TO YOU THEN, SO WHY DOES THAT MEAN ANYTHING NOW?!"

Derricka was furious.

"You're right. But I'm more than asking you; I'm begging you to forgive me."

"What part do you want me to forgive you for? The part where your husband made me suck his dick, or spread my legs every night after I put the girls to bed?"

Derricka watched her mother fall to the ground from the shock of her words.

"Derricka, he made you do what? Oh God no. Please no, all of you?!"

"No mama just me, I look like you the most, Plus I am the oldest, so I was more developed."

Derricka continued, "I cried for you to come home every night, but you never came. It took for me to slice him from ear to ear for him to stop molesting me."

"This is all my fault, I should have been there. I wouldn't have let him hurt you… any of you."

"Well mother you weren't there, and he did hurt me, so it's too late for should have, could have, would have's."

"I deserve to feel all this anger you have towards me, but please don't make my life any worse than it is by not forgiving me. It took forever for me to realize that my dreams of being a well-known artist meant nothing without my girls."

"Artist? I don't remember you being artistic." Derricka stated.

"Because your father said being an artist was stupid, they never made any money, and that we didn't have the time or funds to pursue petty childhood dreams. I drew and painted in secrecy. No one has ever seen my work."

She walked over to her cart and pulled out an old worn down briefcase.

"I drew this picture of you when you were sleeping." Derricka took the picture and was amazed at the detail and skill of the drawing.

"I used to send hand-made birthday and holiday cards, along with letters with drawings attached to tell you girls how much I loved and missed you, but none of you ever responded back."

"Mama we never saw any cards or letters. Dad didn't allow us to get the mail. He always walked in the door with it." Derricka said frowning.

"I figured that, but that never stopped me from writing to you girls."

She handed Derricka a bundle of letters.

"I want you to read these…you and your sisters. Your father wouldn't take me back. He said that he had someone new. I didn't know that person was you."

"Mama I'm sorry. It was just horrible without you. I really, desperately needed you."

"I know baby, and that's why I'm just asking you to try to find it in your heart to forgive me. I'm not asking for us to be best friends overnight, but just to give our mother and daughter relationship a chance."

"That's why I came here looking for you, actually." Derricka handed her mother a tissue.

"Look mom, a lot has been going on in my life. I'm happier than I've ever been. I love my career, my friends, and my wonderful man, but I knew in my heart that if I didn't make amends with you, I'd still find some way to feel unfulfilled. What I'm saying is, I came here to tell you that I do forgive you, and would like for us to get to know each other. I just let those painful memories steer me away from my purpose of coming to find you."

"Derricka do you mean that?"

"Yeah mom, I truly mean that."

Her mother used the tissue she wiped her tears with to wipe her daughter's.

"God is good. Let me grab my cart and we can go by the water and talk."

Derricka pushed the cart away.

"No, you won't need any of these things anymore. Both of us are going to start brand new and leave the past in the past."

"That sounds wonderful, but I want you to take me to see your father. I think he and I need to talk."

Chapter Twenty Three

Nothing can tear us apart

Ethan couldn't believe that this early in their relationship, he was thinking about marriage. He knew without a doubt that Brooklyn was his future wife. He watched her smell his scent from the t-shirt he wore the previous night. He was just about to head in her direction when his phone rang.

"What's up?"

"Ethan we know you don't come in until tomorrow, but we need you now! There's a huge fire in Forest Park on Lake Street."

"Okay I'm on my way." Ethan hung up disappointed.

"Baby there's a big fire, and the crew needs me. I have to go."

"Okay, but please be careful! I love you."

But the door slammed before he said I love you back.

****

Ethan pulled up to a chaotic scene. His captain brought his fire suit with them, so that Ethan could change when he got there.

"Ethan! Hurry up kid. Put on your suit!" yelled the captain.

Ethan quickly dressed and ran to the group.

"Okay there is three children trapped on the fourth floor. The floors and ceilings are beginning to collapse. I don't know how the hell the parents made it out without grabbing their children, but they did. I need you, Mike, and Chris to go get those babies. The rest of us will try to kill the flames." said the captain.

He gave instructions to the three men, then sent them off to complete the mission. It was black and difficult to maneuver through the burnt wood and debris, but Ethan managed to lead the men to the third floor safely. Just as they were climbing the stairs to the fourth floor, the staircase collapsed and Mike fell through to the second floor.

"Mike! Mike can you hear me?!" Ethan screamed.

"Chris go down there and get him out of here!" Chris nodded his okay, and followed orders. Ethan carefully made his way to the fourth floor. He could hear a child crying. When he approached the room, he saw a little boy passed out on the floor, and a boy and girl hugged closely at the window.

"Hey there, my name is Ethan. I'm here to take you to your mommy and daddy. Will you let me do that?"

"Yes, I'm ready to go." said the little boy.

Ethan wrapped cold wet towels around the children. He had the girl climb onto his back, he put one boy over his shoulder, and carried the other one in his arms.

"Okay everybody stay under the towel and keep your heads down, okay?"

Lord please let me get these babies out of here. Please, Ethan thought. He was able to dodge falling wood, and the holes in the floor all the way to the second floor. Ethan took a wrong turn and ran into the blaze. He tried to go back in the direction he came from, but the ceiling completely collapsed. He grabbed his radio and told the captain to raise the ladder to the second floor window, because they were trapped.

"Sure thing Ethan, it's being raised now."

Chris stood at the top of the ladder reaching towards Ethan.

"This one was passed out when I got him, so take him first."

Chris passed the boy to another fireman and went back up to grab the other little boy.

"Okay honey, he's coming back for you, and you'll get to see the paramedics and all their cool equipment." said Ethan.

"Are you coming?"

"Yes, I'll be right behind you. What's your name baby girl?"

"Kennedy."

"That's such a pretty name."

She gave Ethan a hug before she climbed into Chris's arms. Ethan was about to climb out when he was hit in the head by a large piece of wood, knocking him out.

"Oh shit! I think Ethan's hurt! Chris get back on that ladder and see if you see him!"

Chris tried to spot Ethan but all he could see was flames and smoke.

"Boss I can't see him!"

"Shit! I'm going in there." said the captain.

****

It had been a few hours since Brooklyn had seen or talked to Ethan, and she was starting to get concerned. Why am I tripping? He's a fireman. These things take time. You don't put out a fire in a matter of seconds, thought Brooklyn. A knock on the door interrupted her thoughts.

"Who is it?!"

"Derri."

"Hey boo, come on in..."

Brooklyn thought she was hallucinating. It was like seeing how Derricka would look when she got older.

"Brooklyn, this is my mother. Mom this is my best friend Brooklyn."

"She's as beautiful as you and Aaron said."

"Why thank you ma'am. Come in please."

Brooklyn opened a bottle of wine, and the three of them talked, laughed, and cried.

"I always said I wish I had Derri's heart. I can't see me and my mother reconciling."

"Just pray on it baby. I did and today my prayer was answered."

Brooklyn fell silent.

"Brooklyn are you okay?" asked Derricka.

"Ethan rushed out of here hours ago, because he received a call about a large fire in Forest Park. I haven't heard from him and I'm kind of worried."

"BK he's a strong man. He's fine. He'll call any minute now." said Derricka.

"I hope so Derri. I hope so."

****

The captain climbed through the window and tripped over Ethan's foot.

"Ethan!"

He checked for a pulse, but didn't feel one. I'm too old to try to carry a grown man, thought the captain. He leaned out of the window.

"Chris, help me get him down this ladder!"

They carried Ethan to safety, and laid him on the ground.

"Paramedics, get your asses over here and work on my fireman!"

And that's exactly what they did.

"Well captain we got him breathing, but he's barely with us. The blow to his head is serious, so we have to get him to the hospital and fast."

"Well I'm riding with him." said the captain.

When they arrived at the emergency room, the captain called Joe.

"Okay now I'm starting to worry. Maybe you should call him instead of waiting." said Derricka.

"That's a good idea. Your mom is knocked out. Maybe you should get her home." Brooklyn suggested. Brooklyn walked her guests to the door and was startled by Joe when she opened it.

"Joe what are you doing here?"

"Brooklyn we have to go to the hospital. Ethan was seriously hurt in the fire."

Brooklyn was frozen.

"Brooklyn get your keys and go. I'll drop mom off and meet you guys there." Derricka said.

"Joe what hospital is he at?" asked Derricka.

"He's at Rush Oak Park. Brooklyn we have to hurry."

So many things were going through Brooklyn's mind. Could she stand to see Ethan lying in a hospital bed? Will this ordeal bring them closer together…or push them apart?

"We're here." said Joe.

Brooklyn was reluctant to go inside, but Joe grabbed her hand and led her to the front desk.

"Hello Miss, we're looking for a patient named Ethan Palmer." said Joe.

Brooklyn was growing impatient, because the lady was more interested in stuffing her face than looking Ethan up on the computer.

"Could you put the damn sandwich down and find my man!"

"Your man was taken to surgery, so you can't see him now anyway."

Joe stopped Brooklyn from punching the lady in the face.

"Joe I' ma work her ass out! She better get right."

"Joe, Brooklyn..." The captain came into the waiting room.

"Oh Captain what happened to him." Brooklyn asked.

"He saved three small children from the fire, but was hit in the head by a large piece of wood. It knocked him out and caused some swelling on his brain. He's in surgery as we speak. I've been keeping the crew up to date. They all should be here shortly."

The captain handed Brooklyn and Joe cups of coffee as they sat in silence. Only an hour had passed, but it felt like an entire day.

"Are you the family of Ethan Palmer?"

"Yes doctor, we are. How is he?" asked Brooklyn.

"I'm doctor Carrington, and he's in recovery right now. The surgery was a success. We were able to drain all of the excess fluid from his brain."

"When will we be able to see him, doctor Carrington?" asked Joe.

"You can see him once he's removed from recovery, and placed in a room. Tonight is very critical for him, so he could use your prayers. Now it is a good thing that he's breathing on his own, but if he doesn't wake up from the anesthesia soon, that can mean he's slipped into a coma." Brooklyn gasped.

"Now I'm not trying to scare you, but comas can be very unpredictable. Some people are in comas for days, and some for years. I'm wishing for a speedy recovery. If you have any questions or concerns, I'm here all night. Just have the front desk page me."

"Thank you doctor, please keep us informed." said Joe.

Brooklyn grabbed Joe and the Captain's hands.

"I think we should pray like the doctor said."

Chapter Twenty Four

The apple doesn't fall far from the tree

"Mom I'm meeting up with Brooklyn. I'll check on you later!"

"Derricka, just a second."

"Yea, what's up?"

"What's your father's address?"

"Mom what are you up to?"

"Nothing baby. I just want him to see that I still look good."

"He's still in our old house…well that's what Janine said."

"Janine still talks to your father after what he did to you?"

"Yep. That's why she's nonexistent to me. I don't deal with disloyalty."

"I understand, but you forgave me though; give it time. Call me and let me know how Brooklyn's holding up."

"I will mom. Lock up."

She watched as her daughter pulled off and turned the corner.

"I'm sorry Derri baby, but I'm about to pay your father a rude visit." She took the spare key from the flower pot and began her walk to 1809 W. Linder.

****

Brooklyn called Derricka and asked her to meet at her apartment. Derricka arrived and took a deep breath before knocking on the door. Ethan is alright Derricka, why are you so anxious, she thought.

"Who is it?"

"It's me, BK."

When Brooklyn opened the door, Derricka could see on her face that Ethan was obviously not alright.

"Hey Hon how is he?"

Brooklyn wrapped her arms around her best friend and broke down.

"Brooklyn, oh my God is Ethan okay?"

"He's in a coma. What am I supposed to do Derri? I love him." Brooklyn said crying.

"Listen to me, Ethan is a fighter, literally. This will not beat him. He will wake up the same amazing man he always was. Look at me BK. You have to be strong for him, because he needs you."

"You're right. I'm taking a leave from work, and I'm not leaving his side until he opens his eyes and responds to me."

"You don't have to do this alone. I'm sure we all can take shifts. You, me, Joe, Aaron, and Thailand.

Brooklyn giggled, "Thailand? He can't peel himself from Adriana for five seconds."

"Yeah they're out of town."

"Again?! Where are they now?" asked Brooklyn.

"The Bahamas. They sent us an email full of pictures."

"I'm hungry. Let's cook up some stuff and get drunk."

"Sounds like a plan." Derricka agreed.

****

I see he still has those ugly curtains up, thought Derricka's mom. She rang the doorbell without thinking twice. He opened the door.

"Well I'll be damned. Look who stopped by. What brings you here Leslie?"

"I was in the neighborhood, so I decided to see if you were still alive. Looks like you almost didn't make it." Leslie said pointing to the scar that stretched from one ear to the other. He stared at her and rubbed his keloid scar.

"Well come in, and take a load off."

Leslie was amazed at how the house was the same way she left it. Same furniture, same colors, even the same vases and lamps.

"Janine baby, come out here. We have a surprise visitor."

"Who is it daddy?"

Janine walked into the living room surprised to see her mother sitting on the sofa.

"Mom? What are you doing here?"

"The question is Janine, what are YOU doing here?"

"I'm where I belong. This is not your man or house anymore…both are mine now."

"You nasty bastard! Having sex with your daughters! You will burn in hell for this!"

"I'm sorry for doing those things to Derricka. I crossed a line that a parent should never cross. I broke her virginity, taught her how to handle me…the same way I did with you. She looked so much like you. She was the closest thing I had to you. I wish I could take all of it back, but Janine and I just kind of happened. I didn't mean for it to be this way."

"Both of you are sick and disgusting! You are so lucky your perverted ass can't be locked up for this. And you little girl..." Leslie walked up to Janine, "Should be ashamed of yourself. He molested your sister for years! And you're sleeping with him willingly?!"

"Bitch you left us! We had to fend for ourselves! You didn't..."

"YOU DIDN'T FEND SHIT! DERRICKA COOKED, CLEANED, PLAYED MOMMY AND WIFEY

IN THIS HOUSE! YOU DIDN'T DO A DAMN THING!"
Enraged, Leslie knocked over a lamp before smacking her
daughter.

"George, smacking you won't be satisfactory
enough. I have something else for you."

She pulled out a tape recorder.

"I have everything that was said on tape. You're an
eighth grade teacher. Once I make copies of this tape, along
with your photo, you won't be able to work with children
EVER AGAIN!"

Janine's mouth dropped. Leslie left crying uncontrollably.
This nasty bastard is about to pay, thought Leslie. She
made it back in the house just in time to answer Derricka's
call.

"Hello?"

"Hey mom, I'm not coming home tonight, Ethan,
unfortunately is in a coma, so I don't want to leave BK's
side right now."

"Oh I understand baby. Be there for your friend. I'll
be fine."

"Okay good night."

"Good night Derri and I love you."

"Love you too mom."

Leslie hung up, poured herself a glass of wine, and started working on the computer. This is the least I can do for my baby, Leslie thought while looking at Derricka's photo.

****

"Janine your mother is right. This is wrong. We shouldn't be doing this."

"Fuck her! She's just jealous because you didn't want her or Derricka. I'm better than them."

Janine reached over to kiss her father on the lips, but he pushed her away.

"Janine stop it! I'm ending this. I need help. WE need help. This isn't right."

"Mothafucka when did you get a conscience?" The Pain and agony you put Derricka through was ridiculous! The screams, the moans, the banging of the headboard. THE ONLY THING YOU DID RIGHT WAS WEAR A DAMN CONDOM!"

"Get out of my house Janine."

"I'm not going no damn where! All the time I put into you. I'm not dumb. I saw the way you were looking at her. YOU WANT HER BACK! But why? She left us! If you think you are going to leave me for her, you have another thing coming."

Janine grabbed a vase and smashed it across her father's head, knocking him out cold.

"I'll teach that bitch to come up in here and try to ruin my happy home. There's only one place she can be, and that's Derricka's house." She grabbed a butcher's knife out of the kitchen, blew her father a kiss, and left for Derricka's house.

Chapter Twenty Five

Things happen for a reason

Derricka called Aaron over to keep her and Brooklyn company; they discussed taking turns monitoring Ethan throughout the day and night.

"BK I talked to Thailand, and he and Adriana are returning early from their trip to be here for you and Ethan." said Aaron.

"Aww Aaron, they don't have to do that."

"Yes we do. You and Ethan are an important part of our lives." said Derricka.

"I love you guys. I'm exhausted, so I'm going to crash. Visiting hours start at 9 A.M. I want to be there by 8:30."

"No problem. Goodnight boo." said Derricka. Derricka had been waiting for a moment to be alone, so she could cry herself. She struggled to stay strong in front of Brooklyn, because her best friend is devastated. She buried her head in Aaron's chest and began to weep.

"Baby all of this will be over soon. Ethan is going to wake up and live like he never left."

"I know it's just hard to see her hurting like this. She really loves this man. He's everything she's ever wanted. "I'm so glad that's not you lying in a coma. I don't think I would make it."

"I'm not going anywhere. Believe that." said Aaron.

****

Janine pulled up to Derricka's place with malicious intent. She'd followed Derricka here countless times and prayed for a reason to run up in there and wreck shop. She wanted to get rid of her mother, and this time for good. She rang the doorbell and waited for her mother to open the door.

"Who's there?"

"It's Janine mom. I just came by to apologize." When Leslie opened the door, Janine forced her way inside, breaking Leslie's nose. Bent over in pain, Janine kicked Leslie down and sat on top of her.

"Bitch did you really think I came here to apologize?" Janine removed the butcher's knife from her purse.

"You think you can just come into our lives after all these years, and judge us?"

Leslie tried to sit up, but Janine punched her in the nose.

"Aww mommy, did that hurt? I hope it did! You know what hurt a lot mama? When you left us…that's what hurt a lot. What makes you think you're going to get daddy back?"

"I don't want your nasty ass daddy! That's why I left in the first place." Leslie said choking on blood.

"I worked hard to get him! I had to wait until he got over Derricka. I wanted to kill her for slicing my daddy like that, but it worked out for me, because after that he let her go."

"You're just as sick as your father. I should've aborted you like I started to."

Janine kicked her in the side.

"FUCK YOU LADY! BECAUSE OF YOU HE WANTS TO END THINGS BETWEEN US! But I can't let that happen. You and your precious Derricka have to go!" Janine sat back on top of Leslie and raised the knife above her head. Before she could stab her mother, Leslie slid a pen out of her pocket and jammed it into Janine's neck, causing blood to splatter across the wall. Leslie scrambled to get the phone. She was dizzy from all the blood she was losing, but she managed to dial 911 and then Derricka's cell.

"Derricka she tried to kill me…she tried…to kill me."

"WHO MAMA, WHO?"

"Janine...she... and your father…are lovers."

"Mama try to stay with me okay? Don't hang up until the paramedics come."

Derricka didn't hang up until she heard the voices of two men on the other end of the phone. She told Aaron and Brooklyn what happened and they sped to the hospital.

"Excuse me nurse, I'm looking for Leslie Fallon."

"Oh she's over there talking to those officers." The nurse pointed to the second room from the desk.

"Are you okay Mom?! What the hell happened?!" questioned Derricka.

"This is your daughter? Well how many do you have?" asked one officer.

"I have four. The one that tried to kill me is Janine, my youngest daughter."

One of the officers asked Derricka about the phone call she received from her mother, and other questions about her father and sister.

"Did you know that your father and sister were intimate?"

"No, no I did not."

"Did you know that your mother was going to your father's home?" asked the officer.

"No I didn't."

"Okay well do you know why your sister would want to kill you and your mother?"

"ME?! Why does she want to kill me?"

"Well according to your mother, Janine was jealous of your relationship with your father, and she felt like you two were trying to break them up."

"Where's Janine now?"

"She was admitted in here as well. Your mother stabbed her in the neck. I don't know her status."

"Thank you officer."

Derricka met up with the others and explained what happened.

"That's crazy!" said Aaron.

"Yeah who are you telling?" Derricka said.

"Y'all better not be talking about my broken nose."

"Mom, you're okay… thank God."

"Yep, but your sister isn't. The doctor just informed me that due to the amount of blood she lost, she's going to need a blood transfusion, and even if I was a match I wouldn't give her a drop of my blood."

"Let them ask daddy. That bitch wanted to kill me anyway. Let's go." said Derricka.

As they were walking out of the hospital, Brooklyn received a call from Joe.

"Hey, Joe, what's going on?"

"He's awake Brooklyn, and he's asking for you."

"I'm…I'm on my way! Aaron drop me off at Rush Oak Park. Ethan's awake."

****

Brooklyn ran into the hospital and damn near fell over the desk.

"Whoa, slow down ma'am. How may I help you?"

"I need a visitor's pass for Ethan Palmer."

"Here you go. He's in his room giving the nurses hell."

"Ethan, baby." Brooklyn instantly began to cry.

"Hey bay, I want to go home."

"Okay, I'm going to take you home. I'm so happy that you're awake."

"I was just tired baby. I needed a nap."

"A nap?" Brooklyn asked laughingly.

"Yeah a nap. I love you Brooklyn. I know one day you're going to be my wife."

"I know I will be too."

"Well why do you two have to wait until one day?" asked Joe.

Joe went into his jacket pocket and pulled out a ring box.

"I always wanted to have a wife. I lied all of these years, just pretending to be married, because I knew I screwed over a lot of good women. I bought this ring two decades ago, and now I'm passing it to you, son."

Ethan opened the box to find an antique ruby ring.

"Brooklyn would you please be my wife?"

"Yes! Yes I will."

He slid the ring on her finger and passionately kissed her. Joe sat back and watched their faces glow with love. It was bittersweet for him. On one hand On one hand he was happy his son had found love…something that he'd regretted turning his back on in the past. On the other hand, he realized that if you are sincere with your words and sincere in your actions, put God first in your life, and be real with yourself at all times...then forgiveness comes easy, and love...Well love wouldn't be that complicated.

EPIOLOGUE

Aaron was standing outside of Derricka's apartment when she overheard him talking to Thailand on the phone about Ethan's accident. She'd been following him, Derricka, and the entire crew for weeks, snapping pictures, taking notes, while devising a plan to get Thailand all to her-self like he promised. She was right there in the crowd of spectators when Ethan ran into that burning building for the children. She hoped to God that Ethan didn't make it out unharmed, because she knew that Thailand would show up for support, and this would be her chance to confront him. She cracked a slight smile at the fact that she would get the chance to give him an ultimatum. Either stop sleeping with all of these sluts and be with her or risk having everything he's ever loved ripped out of his life.

She reclined the driver seat, closed her eyes and began to masturbate at the thought of having Thailand inside of her. Imagining him on top of her made her clit throb like a heartbeat. She couldn't take it; she had to have him again. She moaned uncontrollably as she fingered her-self until her body jumped and jerked, screaming Thailand's name as she climaxed.

"For his sake and theirs, I hope he makes the right decision."

She pulled up her panties and drove off, licking her juices off her middle and index finger.

The sequel to Climatic Successions

Catch 22

(Love's Paradox)

      Adriana hadn't slept in days. Thailand hadn't returned any of her texts or phone calls, and Aaron's status hadn't changed. Since the day she could hold a paintbrush, Adriana had painted her pain until she couldn't muscle up the strength to stroke any longer. She put her hair in a ponytail and pulled a stool up to a blank canvas. A heart shattered into pieces is what she felt and so she would paint. Short or long, every brush stroke helped her breathe a little easier. A knock at the door startled her, causing her to drop the paint brush onto her pants.

      "Shit. WHO IS IT?!" she yelled.

      "Hello, I'm looking for Ms. Adriana Jackson?" the voice on the other end said.

      "I'm sorry, but the gallery isn't open today, Tuesday through Saturday only." Adriana stated, annoyed by the interruption.

"Oh I know. I was hoping to talk to her about creating a painting for a special friend of mine; Aaron." Well shit, now I have to open the door, thought Adriana.

"Hi, I'm Adriana."

"Yes, I know. I've always wanted to meet you. Your work is well known all over Chicago. It is an honor."

"Thank you. Please come in."

You're going to regret this. Once I'm done with you, no one will be able to recognize you, the visitor thought.

"So how do you know Aaron?" Adriana wanted to know.

"I'm a regular at his restaurant. The menu and entertainment are exquisite, can't get enough of the place."

"Yea his place is one of the best in all of downtown Chicago. I take it you two are pretty cool?"

"Oh yea, we share a passion for art. He never shut up about his all-time favorite painter, Ms. Adriana Jackson. After hearing about his tragic accident, couple of the other regulars and I thought it would be nice to chip in and ask you to create an exclusive piece to hang inside his restaurant."

"That is so sweet. Of course I will create a piece on you guys' behalf. It will be free of charge."

"Oh no! You don't have to do that. We are more than willing to pay you for your services, Ms. Jackson."

"No, no I insist. What concept did you all come up with?"

"Well we all thought that whatever you came up with would be fitting. Your work is known for exuding strength through pain, triumphs over tribulations, persevering through the storm; you know things of that nature. I think you should paint like it's your very last time. It just might be."

"What do you mean by...?" Pain rushed through Adriana's head like a freight train. Dizzy with blood dripping in her eyes, she tried to get up off the floor.

"Who...who are you?"

"Who am I? When you opened that door, I became the worst decision you've ever made, that's who I am!" She struck Adriana again, causing her to black out. Standing over her, she began to go off into a rant.

"You think you can just bat those exotic green eyes, and walk around Chicago like you're the shit! You and Thailand MAKE ME SICK! Always hugging and kissing, taking trips around the world, and smiling in everybody faces." She kicked Adriana before continuing her rant.

"You think you are going to reap what I sewed?! I DON'T THINK SO! That's okay, either he's going to give me what I want or I'm getting rid of your ass. LET'S SEE HOW MUCH HE REALLY LOVES YOU!" She tossed the wrench she used to hit Adriana with across the room, and then she began dragging her towards the back door. She put Adriana in the trunk of her car and went back to clean up the few specs of blood that spilled. You better hope he complies with my demand or else you will never paint again, she thought. She drove to a remote area an hour outside of Chicago and parked on the side of an abandoned house. As she was tying Adriana's wrist behind her back, she began to awake.

"Where... Am... I?" Adriana was disoriented.

"You wouldn't know if I told you."

"Why am I here? Why are you doing this?"

"You ask a lot of questions. Do you always talk this much?" Tightening the knot on the rope, she continued…

"Do you love Thailand?"

"Yes." answered Adriana.

"You think he loves you?"

"Yes."

"Really? Well we shall see."

"What do you want from me?"

"It's not you that I want something from. It's him. He owes me, and it's time to pay up."

"How much? I'll pay you. Just tell me how much and it's yours." Laughing she smacked Adriana across her naïve face.

"Like I said! He owes me, not you!" She force fed Adriana some pills and poured water down her throat.

"Bottoms up bitch."

"What the hell did you just give me?"

"Just a little something to keep you calm and relaxed, now I'll be back to check on you later, don't bother screaming. No one will hear you." Adriana watched her abductor leave the barn. Minutes later she heard a car start and then drive away.

"Oh my God Thailand, what have you gotten us into?"

Before driving off she took out a sheet of paper and an envelope. She wrote twelve words, put the note in the envelope, and sealed it with a kiss.

"How deep is your love Thailand? We are about to find out." She sped off smiling at the fact that what she's waited on for so long will be hers sooner than later. She parked a few house down from his.

"I can't wait to see the look on his face when he reads this." She said to herself. Carefully, but swiftly she placed the letter on his front porch and rang the doorbell. Thailand looked out the window to see no one outside. He opened the door thinking that maybe some bad ass kids were trying to ruffle his feathers for fun. He spotted the envelope and picked it up. "Another one?" he said aloud. The contents of the note made him do a double take as his heart instantaneously dropped.

"If you ever wanna see her again, you'll give me what's mine."

"Oh my God…Adriana." Thailand looked around one last time but didn't see anyone. He went inside and immediately called Ethan.

"Yo E, I got another one."

www.ingramcontent.com/pod-product-compliance
Lightning Source LLC
Chambersburg PA
CBHW060317050426
42449CB00011B/2519